JUDSON PRESS

PUBLISHERS SINCE 1824

I've Been
Called
Now What?

Adam L. Bond
Foreword by Stephen Lewis

JUDSON PRESS
PUBLISHERS SINCE 1824

Join our mailing list for updates and special offers.
www.judsonpress.com/mailing_list.cfm

I've Been Called: Now What?
© 2012 by Judson Press
All rights reserved.

Judson Press has made every effort to trace the ownership of all quotes. In the event of a question arising from the use of a quote, we regret any error made and will be pleased to make the necessary correction in future printings and editions of this book.

Unless otherwise noted, Scriptures are quoted from the New Revised Standard Version of the Bible, copyright © 1989 by the Division of Christian Education of the National Council of the Churches of Christ in the United States of America. Used by permission. All rights reserved.

Interior design by Beth Oberholtzer.
Cover design by Wendy Ronga, Hampton Design Group.

Library of Congress Cataloging-in-Publication Data
Bond, Adam.
    I've been called : now what? / Adam Bond ; foreword by TBD. — 1st ed.
      p. cm.
    Includes bibliographical references.
    ISBN 978-0-8170-1711-8 (pbk. : alk. paper) 1. Pastoral theology. 2. Clergy—Appointment, call, and election. I. Title.
    BV4011.4.B66 2012
    253'.2—dc23
                                    2012023066

Printed in the U.S.A.
First Edition, 2012.

Contents

Foreword by Stephen Lewis   vii

Preface   xi

Acknowledgments   xiii

Introduction   xvi

Part One: Considering Ministry

Chapter 1   That Bush Is Burning! God Calls   3

Chapter 2   Find a Mentor—Fast!   14

Chapter 3   Where Charisma Will Not Take You   24

Chapter 4   The Unwritten Rules of Ministry   36

Part Two: Preparing for Excellence in Ministry

Chapter 5   Study to Show Yourself Approved:
            Three Years of Self-Discovery   53

Chapter 6   Considering Ordained Ministry   69

Chapter 7   Where Do I Go from Here?
            Ministry Placement   81

Part Three: Reflecting on Ministry Matters

Chapter 8   Salaries, Service, and Sabbath   97

Chapter 9   Thoughts on Success in Ministry   106

Chapter 10 Nurturing the Next Generation   115

Conclusion   121

Appendixes

Appendix A Sample Interview Questions   123

Appendix B Sample Questions for the Search
Committee   127

Appendix C Sample Church Description   129

Appendix D Sample Cover Letter   130

Appendix E Sample Thank-You Letter   132

Recommended Resources   135

Foreword

Fewer words are associated with mystery than the word *calling*, and fewer are more important for how a Christian minister's life might unfold. I have not met a minister or someone discerning a call to ministry who has not wrestled with his or her sense of calling or what to do in response to being called.

If you are like many faithful and courageous Christian leaders who have been called or who may be accompanying someone else in discerning a call to ministry, this book is for you. While the claims of a calling on one's life are filled with beauty, awe, and fulfillment, a calling can also stir up feelings of fear, anxiety, and uncertainty about what to do next. The author offers answers to the reader asking: What are my next faithful steps in pursuing a call to ministry?

Every year, I work with young adults and with the institutions supporting them in discernment of a call to Christian ministry. Many of the questions—Am I called to pastor, teach, or do something else? Whom do I turn to for guidance? Should I go to school or jump into ministry? How do I find a job in ministry?—that we hear from these young adults are the kinds of questions that are addressed in *I've Been Called: Now What?* In a time when denominational resources on vocational discernment are waning, when networks for mentoring and apprenticeships are limited, and when the process for discerning and securing a position in ministry has become increasingly mysterious and assigned to a few wise sages in the church, the author demystifies the call process and makes it accessible to a wider audience.

In this exciting new book, Adam L. Bond speaks directly to the questions that many of Christ's servants are wrestling with after acknowledging a call to ministry. I have known Adam for several years as a friend, colleague, and fellow with the Fund for Theological Education (FTE). As a scholar in theology, a Christian minister, a leader within a denomination, and as a counselor and mentor to scores of seminarians, Adam offers a wealth of information and wisdom for those exploring the next steps in answering God's call. Bond is honest about the challenges to pursuing God's call and offers helpful suggestions and questions to consider that are instructive for discerning how to become a Christian minister.

Bond reflects on his own experiences of being called and counseled in discerning a call to ministry, and his use of Scripture and examples from the larger culture are effective in illustrating vital points related to the call to ministry. For example, Bond's analogy of team sports as a way to describe one's vocational role within a ministry team underscores the importance of being true to one's vocational identity and particular gifts. His chapter on mentoring reminds us that ministry is not a solo act and that guides along the way can support us in our journey into professional ministry. He helpfully explains some of the basic unwritten rules of ministry that every minister must learn how to navigate.

While Bond underscores that every person's path to ministry is unique and different, I appreciated his chapter "Study to Show Yourself Approve," which suggests the importance of preparing for ministry prior to jumping straight into it and the distinctions between the various ways a person might prepare for ministry. Finally, the chapter "Where Do I Go from Here? Ministry Placement" is particularly good if you are interested in understanding how to navigate the job market in Christian ministry.

Adam Bond offers a wealth of knowledge and does a masterful job of describing what's next after discerning that you have been called. I cannot speak highly enough about the need for such a resource and recommend *I've Been Called: Now What?* as a companion to your discernment process. Read each chapter and spend some time journaling your answers to the questions at the end of each chapter.

I highly recommend this book as well to the family member, friend, or colleague who knows someone who is called or wrestling with a call to ministry and to the spiritual director, professor, mentor, or church leader who is accompanying the next generation of leaders who have answered a called to ministry.

Read this book! You will not be disappointed! It is a must-have resource for leaders exploring the next steps in the journey of becoming a Christian minister in the world.

Stephen Lewis
The Fund for Theological Education

Preface

My students and I sometimes surprise each other with the candid conversations that we share in class. One conversation about "the church" led several of them to lament the lack of mentoring they receive from pastoral leaders and professors. Aha! They had just confirmed a hunch: *New ministers do not always feel confident in their vocational journey.* I volunteered the basic outline of this book as a response to their concerns. "This is the book that I am going to write," I said. Most of the seminarians in the room smiled and celebrated the idea. But I also received an unexpected response. One bright and gifted future professor raised this question: "What qualifies you to write *this* book?"

Her question is valid. You will likely raise the same concern. In fact, I asked myself that question with each chapter. I can only offer you a response that you may approve or dismiss.

This book grows out of my journey in ministry. My call, my early ministry, my denominational service, and my work in the seminary seem to reveal the need for this type of portable mentor. At this point, I have been in ministry nearly twenty years. Questions I asked at various stages of my life and ministry have found their way into this book. They join hands with questions I have fielded from seminarians and ministerial associates during my time as a denominational staff member. Moreover, advice I have received from wise elders resides in these pages. My open door policy at the seminary also keeps me busy refining the vocational guidance I am placing in this text. This book, therefore, is a point of departure—not a closing word.

May God encourage and lead you.

Adam L. Bond
Samuel DeWitt Proctor School of Theology
Virginia Union University
Richmond, Virginia, 2012
Jeremiah 29:11

Acknowledgments

Every book is the product of numerous people. Yes, the author is a primary player, but the people who believe in and support the author are important participants in the process. These persons include family members who make time and space for the author to do the work. A set of friends and family cheer on the author. The editorial staff and publisher approve a proposal and publish the text, giving the book a great vote of confidence. And readers suggest by their purchase the importance of the subject. The audience gives the author a chance to offer *a perspective* on that subject. The persons who purchase and read this book give it, perhaps, its last great investment of time and resources. To all of you, I say thank you.

This project started with my ministry journey. I started in ministry with several conversation partners who helped me clarify my call. They supported me and nurtured my vocational journey. My pastors, (Drs.) Charles E. Thornhill, J. C. Wright, Walker Wright, Terry Thomas, Robert L. Pettis Sr., and Rolen L. Womack, have spent meaningful time in shaping my understanding of ministry. Dr. William Eric Jackson and I have wrestled with the issues of this text for more than twelve years. I have also learned a lot about ministry in a short time from my current pastor, Dr. Kirkland Walton.

I must acknowledge the vocational contributions of my seminary professors, classmates, and friends. These persons have granted me the freedom to think aloud and have continued to push me in ministry. I am indeed grateful to my colleagues at the Samuel DeWitt Proctor School of Theology at Virginia Union University (some of whom were my professors). Thank you for supporting the "new guy." My students have also helped me develop this project, and they are a primary reason for this text. In many meaningful conversations about vocation and the need for mentoring, they have asked in a variety of ways, "Now what?" Aamon and Gabriella Miller read early versions of the text. Their feedback was exciting and helpful. And Price and Laura Davis staged an impromptu party to celebrate the book. A special thank you goes to the region staffs of the American Baptist Churches of Wisconsin and the American Baptist Churches of the South.

A major reason for this work reaching print is that I am a child of the church. My parents, Leon and Loretta Bond, had a lot to do with that. We went to the church, a lot (Leon Jr. and Adrianna can attest to that). I thank you both for your presence in my life. I remain grateful for Greater Mt. Eagle (Racine, WI), Mt. Zion (Madison, WI), Zion (Richmond, VA), and St. Peter (Glen Allen, VA). These Baptist congregations are the foundations and laboratories of my notions of church and ministry.

Rebecca Irwin-Diehl and the Judson Press staff encouraged me from the start. I introduced the concept for this book to Rebecca at the 2008 Orientation to American Baptist Life in Green Lake, WI. She made time to sit with me while taking notes on her legal pad. She could see the vision for the book before it was clear to me. She started the editorial process at that moment. Thank you. Kim Shimer and I had several conversations while I was on the American Baptist staff in Wisconsin. She and I had a *long* conversation about print resources for churches. (She let me talk for forty-six of the forty-eight minutes that we were on the phone.) In her sales and marketing wisdom, she suggested that I write for Judson Press. That opportunity turned into Sunday school curriculum. Five years later we are working together again. Thank you, Kim.

My wife and children are wonderful. For some reason, they provided the space for me to do this writing ministry. Wow! Ronda, Raychel, and Alana, the three of you are the greatest! Now what do we do? Thank you for the "Do not disturb Daddy" time. Please continue to remind me of the blessings of a balanced life.

Introduction

The call to ministry can be one of the most confusing events of one's life. Depending on the person and her or his (I will alternate gender throughout the rest of the book) community of faith, one of the biggest challenges for the newly called minister is discerning a vocational path. "What do I do next?" the newly licensed minister asks.

This book anticipates some of the questions a person has after accepting the call to ministry: Is pulpit preaching the only recognized and viable ministry? When should I be ordained? Should I go to a seminary or a Bible college? The pastor may be an able guide for answering these questions, and the congregation may express certain expectations for the ministerial candidate. This resource, however, casts an overview for the minister at most stages of the journey. *I've Been Called: Now What?* identifies some resources and ideas for conversations about the vocation of Christian ministry. I encourage readers to create time and space for discernment. Vocational clarity is a goal that many of us desire but do not seek, yearn for but do not make a priority.

This book challenges some of the established beliefs about ministry options and questions contemporary notions about the vocational development of ministers. Numerous vocational options and paths are available through which ministers may express their gifts, and ministers need intentional mentors for guidance. These mentors may come primarily from the local faith community. Beyond that there are networks of groups or individuals who can provide further help for ministers. The local congregation and the denomination, moreover, are or should be accountable for ministers' growth. But in many churches unintentional ministry apprenticeships exist. By this I mean that some ministers learn about ministry from watching a ministerial leader. She does not receive any intentional instruction; ministry becomes an imitation of the model before her.

This book is meant to be a portable mentor. I hope it prompts new ministers to ask some things that their pastors may not cover. College advisers may not be familiar with every vocational path and may not be able to provide much more than a bibliography on ministry. This book attempts to fill in the gaps. New ministers hear the call from God, receive a license, and sit on the front pew or in the pulpit to watch the pastor at work. But there is more to ministry than imitation.

This book differs from other works that provide guidance to "associate ministers" or newly called, newly licensed ministers-in-training. I chose not to review at great lengths the nature and substance of the call. Several good resources that emphasize these ideas are already available. I do not focus on how to be a good assistant to the pastor. Instead, I encourage people to see how their vocational formation and development complement pastoral leadership and/or serve the local and larger body of Christ.

This book loosely attempts to present ministers at any stage with a guide for considering what is next in their ministry. Ministers with some years of experience may find more meaning in later chapters. But the whole book can serve as a refresher course on understanding vocation. This book also differs from books that deal with the minister's journey through seminary. While chapter 5 focuses on related matters, this conversation attempts to address other important stages of the minister's life cycle.

The book does respond to several key issues for vocational discernment and formal theological education for the minister. I ask several questions for the reader to consider, such as: What are the arguments for and against going to seminary or a Bible college? How do I choose a seminary? Does seminary only prepare people for the pastorate? The overarching challenge for readers comes in the form of suggestions for developing and using the gifts God gave them. I hope to provide each reader an opportunity to see the whole board as a good chess player does—that is, see one move/decision in light of anticipated goals.

Newly called ministers need a resource, a portable mentor, to help them think through some of the questions that arise during their journeys. Even with supportive mentors, new ministers benefit from a resource book or person to start conversation(s) about their vocation. Ministers' days are filled with pressures that may overwhelm them without the right support and guidance. Even if they can navigate alone the stressors of a pastorate, chaplaincy, or seminary professorate, why would they not want to seek out a conversation partner? This text, in theory, provides a partner.

The following ten chapters highlight crucial areas of vocational development and provide brief insights into various aspects of the minister's journey. I challenge newly called ministers to give some thought to the landscape of ministry. My hope is that people who are called to ministry will use the book as a guide. And with guide in hand, these ministers-in-training or new ministers can think intentionally about a vocational path, forming checklists to assess their gifts and the vocations that fit them. Ministers-in-training may also find in this book a map for identifying important financial, spiritual, and emotional health resources.

Part One starts with a foundational idea: God calls people to serve humanity. I then reflect on certain narratives—biblical and contemporary—that show God's desire to share meaningful work with humanity for the common good. I provide models for affirming the authentic tug on the heart and mind that many people feel. (You are not crazy; God calls you.) I also recommend websites, books, and articles that encourage ministers to listen and discern.

Throughout the pages of this book, I stress the importance of mentors for supporting new ministers. A mentor is one of the most important people ministers can have in their corner. Developing a relationship with a person who models what God expects of us is a good step in ministry formation. I invite readers at any stage in ministry to consider the value of this practice. Biblical narratives give us a hint at what these relationships provide for the apprentice (e.g. Naomi and Ruth, Moses and Joshua, Elijah and Elisha, not to mention Jesus and his disciples). The mentor can be a guide, advocate, and friend for the newly called/licensed minister. Advocacy can range from presenting opportunities for the new minister to exercise ministry gifts to providing pointers and tips for excelling in ministry.

Part Two begins a conversation on ministry preparation. I celebrate the gifts that people bring to ministry by recognizing what God does in each person God calls. The goal of this section is to consider the urgency of preparation for ministry. I challenge new ministers to celebrate their gifts *and* refine them. Numerous resources are available for helping ministers to identify their gifts and think about their passions. New ministers often need time to reorient their gifts for the new paths they travel. Personality and vocational tests can help with this process. Depending on one's denomination, seminary and the path to ordination are opportunities to learn from such tests and resources. As a seminary professor, I do not shy away from recommending formal theological education.

Part Three addresses some "nuts and bolts" matters of ministry. I address indirectly one important question: If I give myself to the work of ministry, how will God provide for me? The quality of our understanding of ministry and our ministry relationships will help determine those provisions. Who are your colleagues and accountability partners? How do they push you to excellence? For ministry placement, this question is very important. Salaries and ministerial compensation packages also matter to ministers. Denominational resources and assistance from ministry agencies can help ministers place all of these topics in perspective.

To be sure, I raise other important issues. While one finds increasing numbers of women in pulpits, the number of women senior pastors is not equal to the number of women equipped and called to do the work. A pressing need exists for the development of young people in our congregations and communities. What would the world look like if we created a culture in which young people could hear God clearly? How would the world be different if believers would choose their vocational paths with service for God to humanity in mind?

So many questions led me to write this book. As I encounter more and more students, I hear statements about goals and visions for ministry that make me curious about prevailing notions of success. In the final chapter, therefore, I examine competing visions of ministry excellence. One version measures that excellence through numbers of people in pews, preaching engagements, surplus church budgets, and popularity. The other version seeks qualitative measurements. *The goal* is the number of lives changed for the better. This chapter challenges the reader to consider her or his response to this question: How do I define success in ministry? Church growth literature seems to muddy the water on this matter. Expectations from persons in the pews may do the same. But these questions are ours to answer: Is success a megachurch (a big house) and/or a large salary? Or is success the development of people who embrace and practice the values and teachings of Jesus the Christ? Are the two mutually exclusive? I intend for these thoughts to provoke dialogue among colleagues, peers, mentors, and apprentices.

I want to have this conversation about ministry with you. *I've Been Called* is an opportunity to have a meaningful dialogue about the ways in which we construct and define the minister's journey. The book is a type of guide, not a binding contract. *I've Been Called* will not list a prescribed path. But it suggests some modes of transportation. Share it with others and see where the conversation will lead. I hope that the conversation(s) that this book sparks will prompt us to pay close attention to God's voice.

PART ONE

Considering Ministry

CHAPTER 1

That Bush Is Burning!
God Calls

One of the most exciting yet confusing times in a believer's life comes with a call to ministry. The call to a church-related vocation is a celebrated event in the life of a local congregation. Christians generally are happy when they see a brother or sister in Christ accept God's call. The pastor announces it to the congregation in Sunday's morning worship. The people respond with a shout of affirmation, "Amen!" A date is set for an examination and initial sermon. But what happens after that? At this point, confusion can set in for the newly called minister. Will the pastor ask me to sit in the pulpit? Will there be a training session for sitting in the pulpit? How do I do the morning altar prayer? Are there special words that I need to recite during the offertory moment? Will I be a pastor? How do I become a pastor? Is the pastorate the only ministry? These are some of the questions that I asked when I sensed a call to ministry. I still encounter these questions from my students.

In this chapter, I deal with these questions by placing the call of the minister within its two primary contexts: personal experience and the biblical tradition. God calls, you answer. Defining the call and sharing models of call narratives may help the newly called minister gain some perspective on this matter.

What Is a Call?

A call is that unique demonstration of God's desire to work with you in service to humanity. Vocation is another way to express this notion of call. *Vocare* means to call. In the Christian tradition it is God's communication, inviting us to service. Through your vocation or call, God leads you to express *your* gifts, in *your* unique way, in service to people who share the air you breathe. You may fill one of several biblically affirmed ministry positions to do this. For example, as Paul wrote, some are called to be apostles, some prophets, some evangelists, and some pastors and teachers for the work of the ministry (Ephesians 4:11-13). God charges us with the task of discerning and identifying our God-given ministry. We all have gifts that correspond with our ministry calling and the needs that God calls us to meet. Paul talked about the fact that the body has parts that have separate functions for a unified purpose (1 Corinthians 12). The foot is not the hand! The ear is not the eye! It follows, then, that not every person whom God calls will be a pastor, chaplain, or professor.

Team sports may offer us the best analogy for understanding ministry positions. In team sports, coaches assign players to certain positions based on their size and skill level. These positions come with traditional duties attached to them. In basketball the point guard often handles the basketball from one end of the court to the other. She often gives her teammates the signal to set the play into motion and passes the basketball to the open player in the best position to score. The coach, however, may have a different assignment for the point guard. The coach may see in her the ability to score, and the coach may then designate the point guard to do just that. The player has the task of discerning what the coach envisions for her on the court and filling that role. The other players on the team have to do the same thing. They all need one another to take care of the duties that come with their assignments. If they try to be something they are not able to be, they will fail as a unit. But they need each other. No one person is more important than any other person on the team.

There is an unfortunate practice in society wherein people celebrate some players over others based on the positions they play or their duties on the field/court. For example, in basketball we tend to celebrate the scorer more than any other person on the team. What is faulty with this practice is that the person is fulfilling his assignment like all of the other players on the team. He could not do it by himself. The person who captures the rebound and defends the other team well does not have the glamour job, but he is equally important to his team's success. Likewise, the church makes certain positions in its life more glamorous than other positions. We sometimes celebrate the more visible members of "the team" with much fanfare and hoopla while ignoring the essential contributions of the less apparent members. This is something to consider.

God calls people to fill assignments in the body of Christ, the community of believers, both locally and globally. God as creator gives us the gifts and the freedom to develop these gifts and put them into action. God as guide and instructor nurtures us. God places hints and lessons before us that help us clarify our place in the world, the contribution that you or I alone can make. God also allows other people to enter our lives who have keen awareness of matters related to our journeys. Someone may ask, for instance, "Have you ever thought about earning a PhD?" Or someone may say, "You have a real gift for communicating difficult ideas. Have you ever considered a teaching ministry?" A person may hear you preach and recognize your leadership abilities. "You are pastoral material," someone says. Be discerning before you dismiss the comment or run with it.

Or you may be the person with that awareness of others' gifts and potential. I have a cousin who worked for twenty years or more in the United States Postal Service. A few years ago, she noticed more and more that people were looking to her for counsel. She spoke to my mother, who is gifted in discerning vocational matters, about what all of that meant. My cousin prayed about it, talked to her family, and prayed some more. Her period of discernment led her to return to school for a degree in social work.

A social work degree will help her share her God-given gifts. She believes now that she is on the path to living out the call that God has for her life. Note that she is not in full-time parish or congregational ministry. But, she models for us this emphasis on filling an assignment to serve God's people.

Moses, Mary, and You

We can consider Moses' story as a model for discerning the call from God (read Exodus 2–3). Reading the account of Moses' experience at the burning bush helps us draw several conclusions that relate to our thoughts on the call to ministry. Moses was tending the sheep one day for his father-in-law. He came to Mt. Sinai and noticed a burning bush. The fire, however, did not consume the bush. So Moses moved closer to take in this amazing sight. From the bush came a voice with instructions. God called Moses to go and lead the Children of Israel out of Egypt. Talk about an interesting twist to a day. What can we learn from Moses in this story?

First, Moses was observant enough to see the bush burning. Second, Moses was quiet enough to hear God talking through the bush. Third, Moses was sensitive enough to his people's needs to respond to God's call. Consider as well that Moses was conscientious enough to agree with God's assessment of the situation in Egypt. We could go on to talk about his selfless spirit or the courage he demonstrated for his people. That is not the only side of the story. To be sure, he was a flawed hero. Murdering an Egyptian soldier does not seem to be an ideal prerequisite for what God would accomplish through Moses. (God would later direct this same Moses to pen the words "Thou shalt not kill.") But in those early days of the call, Moses resisted, pointing out his own shortcomings to God and asking in essence, "Who am I that the people will listen to me?" When called upon again to work on God's behalf, Moses mentioned his anxieties about his speaking ability. Clearly, Moses was concerned that God was working with the wrong vessel. He considered himself inadequate. Many of us may relate to Moses' attempt to talk God out of a call to ministry. But look at the rest of the story. Moses became a servant leader, leading the people from the bondage of Egypt.

Scripture provides us with other examples of this call and response process. A young woman who was a virgin lived in the town of Galilee. Her name was Mary. The angel Gabriel visited her to share an important message:

Gabriel: God has called you to carry the one who will reign over the house of Jacob. What say you?

Mary: Does God know that my medical history would suggest that I will not be pregnant anytime soon?

Gabriel: Not to worry, Mary, God will take care of the details. Look at your cousin Elizabeth. You do realize how old she is, right? God can make the impossible possible. God will work through you.

Mary: Here I am for service to God. Let it be with me as you have said God will do.

In spite of the physical evidence, Mary was willing to trust that God could work with her.

Your story is probably similar in some ways. You may have had a burning bush type of moment that made you stop in awe of God and God's power. God may have contradicted your idea of how you could give yourself in service to God's will. Or perhaps you just saw that your gifts matched a need—and that was your call. No angelic visitation or extraordinary experience revealed it to you. You just knew that you had something to offer people in a place that lacked what your ministry could give. Whatever the case may be, on a very personal level, God called.

My Story

Among the many resources I had to answer questions about my faith and spiritual journey were my family and church family. The Bonds never missed Sunday school or morning worship. Leon and Loretta Bond made sure that we did not miss much of anything going on when the doors opened to the Greater Mt. Eagle Baptist Church of Racine, Wisconsin. Mt. Eagle gave me my first experiences in front of congregations. The Easter and Christmas speeches, the Sunday school lesson review, and ministry in the youth usher's guild and choir helped me engage in church life. I could not replace those moments of standing in front of friendly faces wishing me well. I am thankful for those "Amens" that quickly rolled off the lips of mothers in the second pew and deacons at the front.

I also learned a lot from my peers. The careful and scrutinizing eyes of my fellow youth gave me a discriminating sense of genuine spirituality versus performance-based attention grabbing. We sat in the rear when we did not have a duty in the worship experience, and we kept watch on and listened to the adults as they modeled church for us. Although we often filled our mouths with apple Jolly Ranchers and "Mystery Mix" Now and Later candies or whispered about the latest news from our respective schools, we tuned in for the important moments in the service. These experiences became part of a database for developing our Christian practices. We knew who would sneak out back for a cigarette and unkind words about the pastor. We also knew who liked and cared about children. Why do these reflections matter? The local church can be an incubator for seekers, for people trying to encounter God's will for their lives. My personal history with the church led me to my classroom in an ecumenical but American Baptist–leaning seminary in Richmond, Virginia. These moments mattered.

Greater Mt. Eagle gave me my first real encounters with life in a larger Christian community. I learned a lot from standing at the door on third Sundays and singing in the youth choir on second Sundays. My father was ordained a deacon at Mt. Eagle, and my mother restarted a nurses' guild that had been defunct. When my brother told my parents he was ready to be baptized while we were at Mt. Eagle, I said I was going to be baptized too. We went into the pool on the same day, though my brother's height led the pastor to dunk (immerse) him twice "to be safe."

It was at Mt. Eagle, moreover, that Dr. Charles Everton Thornhill made an impression on my life. (I will say more about Pastor Thornhill in the next chapter.) He is a gifted and wise pastor who provided and continues to display for me a high standard of what ministry means. His sermons caught my attention. They made me want to listen, even at a young age. I signed up to work for the church's tape ministry when I was thirteen. At that time, the person recording the worship sat in the pastor's office with the audio equipment. I had a headset, microphone volume knobs, and "record" and "pause" buttons. My challenge for those Sundays was to pick out the title of the sermon with as much accuracy as I could. Asking the pastor for his sermon title would have been cheating. Mt. Eagle did not print it in the bulletin, so I had to make sure I was tuned in when he announced it.

The Bond family loved Mt. Eagle, and our church family loved us. When we had to relocate due to my father's job, Mt. Eagle honored us with a dinner on our last Sunday. The church was good for me and to me. I wanted to be involved at Mt. Eagle. This was where my notions of church developed. You see, this was church for me. I was fifteen when we moved, however, and church was about to lose its importance in my evolving teenage consciousness.

My sophomore year in high school was more than a transition from the "new kid on the block" status at the school. My parents relocated us from Racine to Madison, Wisconsin, the state capital. Like most teenagers, I wrestled with insecurities and questions about my existence. Questions about clothing style, manners, mannerisms, and relationships all crossed my mind daily. During high school, I also became much more conscious of my vocational future. What am I going to do when I grow up? But fading into the background quickly was my desire to frequent a local church. All of my real friends were in Racine, and Madison was a strange land.

The church my family settled on, the Mt. Zion Baptist Church, was different. The choir did not sound the same. The deacons did not lead the devotion period as they did in Racine. The Sunday school books were different. And I did not know the people.

These factors made it easier for me to disengage. It was hard enough not fitting in at school, but then I had to go to church and feel like I did not fit in there either. Forget it!

With time, however, individuals in the church began to take an interest in me. From Brother (later Deacon) Larry James to Sister (later Reverend) Jackie Lee to the Gaines family, members of the church decided that I would not sit on the sidelines. They were an important part of my adjustment to Madison. I began to feel like Mt. Zion was a church and family for me. The Reverend Orlando McGruder also helped with this process. He placed a target on my back. Every Sunday after worship, he found me and proceeded to interrogate me. He noticed something in me and tried to ignite it. He would occasionally coteach the teen class with Brother James, and he could hear how well my parents and Mt. Eagle had done their job. Reverend McGruder challenged me to participate in the youth ministry. His hook was that I had gifts that the ministry needed. I could be an example, in his words. That was fine at church, because I could avoid him from time to time. But my mother decided to tutor his wife, who was, at that time, working through nursing school. She did not drive, so he would drop her off and pick her up at our home before and after the tutoring sessions. I would hear the same sales pitch, for the most part, each time he came to the house. To be sure, I did not mind. I figured my excuse was simple. Between basketball practice and homework, my life was full. He did not fall for it.

By the time I was sixteen and driving, my life had little room for church. Sunday school and Sunday morning worship attendance was still a requirement. My parents did not give me a choice. But they did not press me about the "extracurricular" church activities. The summer before my senior year changed everything, however.

Reverend McGruder died of a heart attack on June 22, 1993, at the age of twenty-nine. If my memory serves me well, he died shortly before his first wedding anniversary. The words that he had spoken to me became louder in my mind. I still cannot process the image in my head of seeing him lying in the casket. He was too young. He was dead, but his ministry to others and me was not. I could hear Reverend McGruder and God clearer after this traumatic event.[1]

Maybe God Is Tryin' to Tell You Something

If you are familiar with the movie *The Color Purple,* you may remember the church scene. Margaret Avery's character, Shug, was beckoned to leave a jamboree at the local juke joint by the sound of a gospel choir at her father's church. In a "Hush, somebody's callin' my name" sort of way, the choir's melodies from the church crept on over to the juke joint:

> Can't sleep at night,
> And you wonder why;
> Maybe God is tryin' to tell you something.

She stopped singing the blues tune that was on her lips and began marching toward the church. She joined in with the choir as the words of the gospel song became louder to the crowd that followed her. As Shug continued, she rang out with the line, "I hear ya, Lord!"

Sleepless nights and countless conversations later, I knew what the song meant. I approached my pastors, former and current, to tell them that God was calling me. What did that mean? I needed to look no further than the people whom God had placed in my life from birth to that moment. Several people showed me what it meant to respond to God's call for ministry—Dad and the deacon's ministry and Mom and the nurses' guild, as well as others. Examples of God's servants were always around me. What was I to do? I began to remember how I wrote a sermon at age twelve. This came after hearing my mother preach/speak at a youth day in Zion, Illinois. Was I living into what God had intended for me to do? God was calling. I was ready to answer. The Reverend James Coleman (J.C.) Wright helped guide me through the licensing process. The Mt. Zion Baptist Church licensed me on August 21, 1994. I was eighteen years old. God called, I answered.[2]

Calls Lead You Somewhere, to Someone

My journey did not end with that licensing or even with my first ministry position. I am the product of a call that has led me to various places and people. To be sure, these places were spaces of preparation and ministry. Pastor J. C. Wright believed that God was working in my life. He believed this because he, too, had experienced God move in his life. But he also saw how I gave myself to the places where my gifts matched the church's needs. Even before I was licensed, I felt led to revive the primary class for the Sunday school ministry. I also felt led to volunteer for most of the youth ministry functions—the same youth ministry functions that I avoided the previous year. My call was a call to work where my gifts were needed. The church saw this as well, and the local church licensed me. (As a Baptist, the local church alone has the authority to license and ordain its candidates for ministry.) The church invested in me and affirmed that God wanted me to go and spread the gospel. The congregation's faith in God and me has me in Richmond, Virginia, today and wherever else God may lead me tomorrow.

God's call is to somewhere and to someone. Several biblical characters show us this lesson. Moses returned to Egypt to speak with Pharaoh on behalf of his people. Esther went before the king on behalf of her people. Jonah went to Nineveh to inform the people there of God's concern. In each situation, these individuals served as catalysts for people who needed their leadership. God invested in each of them the gifts and potential to carry out God's will. They had, however, the freedom to choose their course. Moses debated God's choice of ministry agent. Esther had to think about the risk involved for calling in a favor with the king. And Jonah's story illustrates a lesson for those who run from God's call.

In fact, Jonah's call story is a good case study narrative for all of us to ponder (Jonah 1). God calls Jonah to go to Nineveh (somewhere), because of the "wickedness" of its residents (someone). Jonah intentionally pays for fare on a boat that will travel in the opposite direction. During the journey, God sends a violent wind that threatens the voyage. The ship's crew tries to figure out the problem and finds out that the problem's name is Jonah. Jonah tells the crew to throw him overboard, but they do everything in their power to spare a person who seems innocent. The storm gets worse until they finally feel compelled to toss him overboard. One who runs from God's call may have to ask, after reading this narrative, "Am I endangering the productivity, dreams, potential, and—God forbid—the lives of others when I run from God's will?"

God calls. This is evident from the biblical witness, your story, and my story. Not only that, the call will lead you somewhere—to someone. We celebrate that God is willing to work with us to display to other people the love that God revealed to us. And one way we can learn effective ways to do this is through the guidance of a seasoned mentor.

Questions TO CONSIDER

1. When did you notice your call? How did you notice it?

2. What biblical verses or stories encourage you and your sense of call?

3. With whom can you share your call (if you have not already done it yet)?

4. How will you explain this call to your friends and family?

NOTES

1. Sherry Joe, "Rev. Orlando McGruder Jr., 29, Dies of Heart Attack in Wisconsin. He Was Graduate of Wilde Lake," *Baltimore Sun* online, http://articles.baltimoresun.com/1993-06-29/news/1993180067_1_mcgruder-zion-baptist-mount-zion.

2. I am sure that it is no coincidence that three other people who interacted with the Reverend McGruder would later acknowledge calls to ministry and enter seminary.

CHAPTER 2

Find a Mentor—Fast!

Have you seen the movie or read the best-selling book *Tuesdays with Morrie* by Mitch Albom? Albom, a famous Detroit sports columnist, heard about the declining health of a former professor and mentor, Morrie Schwartz, and went to see him. The two reconnected on a very spiritual and human level, much more than a casual sick and shut-in visit. Albom began to visit Morrie weekly, learning from Morrie lessons about life and happiness. These weekly visits were mentoring sessions that gave Albom a "bigger picture" of life's landscape. His rising professional star had led him to mislabel what was important in life. Morrie's guidance showed him that. At the same time, Morrie received something from the relationship as well. He gathered that his life experiences, knowledge, and existence had meaning beyond his brittle frame and a vaporlike time on the earth. To be sure, Albom thought it unfortunate that the most meaningful time that he spent with Morrie was at the close of Morrie's life. In the end, he lamented that he did not have more time with the wise man who helped him resolve some of the deeper questions of his life.

Everyone can benefit from a mentor. I would add to that a sense of urgency: everybody should find a mentor—fast! This is especially crucial in ministry. The minister without vocational clarity risks loss of time in meaningful reflection about her call and in her service to the world. When you know that God is calling you, find that person who models the type of excellence you desire to achieve (in any vocation, not just Christian ministry). A strong mentoring relationship can assist the discerning minister in making sense out of the "bigger picture" questions.

From Being Mentored to Being a Mentor

I have been the beneficiary of wonderful mentoring relationships. From my earliest sense of the call to the present, several people have invested in my vocational development. Nearly every Wednesday, from 2001 through 2008, I would sit at the feet of Dr. Charles Everton Thornhill. He was my childhood pastor and remains a pastor to me regardless of the distance between us. I still call him some Wednesdays to hear his words of guidance and encouragement. Pastor Thornhill would provide me with a checklist of ideas, goals, and concerns to ponder. He would present spaces for me to share my ministry gifts. He supported and encouraged my sense of self as my vision of ministry became a clear call into the classroom.

Another mentor was Pastor Walker Wright, who watched over me during my youthful delusions of grandeur at the University of Memphis. He was an associate director of the Baptist Student Union on campus and is pastor of the White Stone Baptist Church in Memphis, Tennessee. Watching and learning from his character and example gave me conscience-shaping exercises. My road through the academy was lined with professors and pastors who discerned in me the potential and the heart for service in the way I now give. I have found others who have mentored me in different ways, for shorter periods of time, but with a powerful influence. If not for these people investing in me, I do not know where I would be.

The other side of that mentoring relationship has been my responsibility to the people who see *me* as a mentor. There has rarely been a week in a school year where someone has not knocked on my door or sent me an email about a vocational dilemma. "I am not supposed to pastor, but I am not sure what else is out there for me." Or, "Doc, what do I need to do to earn a PhD and teach in a college or a seminary?" One of my students is an excellent writer and motivator. She had an "aha" moment during one of our conversations: "You know what, Dr. Bond, I can write devotional literature. I have a heart for encouraging people." She came to that conclusion after thinking about the ways in which she was already producing devotional messages in her weekly news updates for the church. These are moments that somebody made available for me. A mentor who asks the right questions or makes the time and space available to listen to and explore a minister's deepest questions is a part of the process. Those activities can propel the discerning minister in the direction of a productive ministry. More, then, needs to be said about this mentoring relationship.[1]

What Mentoring Is Not

Dr. Trinette McCray, past president of the American Baptist Churches USA, once shared some insightful information with a group of seminarians from the Samuel DeWitt Proctor School of Theology about vocation and mentoring. Among the brilliant insights she offered was a statement about the expectations of the apprentice or protégé. She shared that some people only look to have mentors who will connect them—instantly—to the mentor's network. Her example implied that the person, who wants to connect with the celebrity preacher, scholar, and the like, wants the mentor to induct him into that celebrity circle as well. The apprentice would thereby take advantage of a connection to the network without the labor of earning respect on his giftedness, integrity, or merit. He is the guy who is with *"the guy,"* so to speak.

I share Dr. McCray's concern about individuals who take that path. It does not reflect the mutual sharing and investment that should exist in the mentoring relationship. In that instance, a person is taking advantage of the mentor for something other than the unique contribution of her person. The mentor is more than a ticket to the big leagues. The mentoring relationship is a covenant (stated or implied) between two people who push each other to struggle with and respond to the questions of identity, vocation, and service in their ministry contexts.

Expectations of Your Ministry Mentor

With a working definition of the mentoring relationship in view, we can identify some key expectations for this relationship. The relationship is one of reciprocity, mutual sharing. The mentor and the protégé learn from each other, gaining from each other a view of the depth of ministry. In mentoring, the mentor receives more from the apprentice than a window into a past that she has forgotten. In other words, the mentor does not just benefit from a reminder of where she was in ministry. The mentor and protégé can and will learn a lot from each other if their expectations are clear. To be sure, this relationship is an investment that keeps both people accountable and grounded in real issues about vocational development and ministry.

The noted performer and songstress India Arie has highlighted well the mentoring relationship in song. In "Better People," she states that older and younger generations can teach and learn from each other. The exchange of values, practices, and technological advice can happen in an encounter between generations. I must admit that even within the same generation, one can learn much from peers about one's vocation. I have benefited from receiving counsel from colleagues who are "in the same boat" with me. Although we find ourselves in similar situations, we have different experiences that may enrich our development through mentorlike sharing. To be sure, we all can provide some type of mentoring. But the key is to have at least a primary person with whom you can share your vocational exploration. What you should expect from that point is a combination of activities that provide you with the guidance that can make vocational clarity possible.

Time

Out of all the things a mentor can do for the protégé or apprentice, the most valuable may be the provision of time to speak with the protégé. Can we quantify that amount? No. Each person has different needs. The wise mentor, however, can discern what that amount of time is based on the varying factors in life. If the mentor is a practicing ministry professional, she cannot give all of her attention to one person's needs. But she can be sensitive to and intentional about the amount of time she allocates for a protégé. Certain situations may require a phone call or email response. Other situations require a lunch or office hour meeting. The developing relationship between these people will help decide which type of response is necessary and how to use that time together.

Patience and Understanding

The mentor should be a patient person. It is likely that the patience the mentor exhibits will be an outgrowth of experience—the result of having been there and done that. A mentor has the ministry experience that we want to acquire in our journey. He can be patient, therefore, knowing from experience the bumps that come with being in ministry. The mentor may also understand that life is a process. One does not receive the sum of one's learning overnight. Those wonderful people who become piano teachers—bless them all—see the bigger picture and understand the steps that come with learning. Notes, finger power, and chord structures take days and years to learn. Many teachers understand and *sometimes* appreciate the awful notes their students play along the way. Ministry is similar to this. The minister cannot learn everything he needs to know at the start of his ministry. Theory and experience come together to create the database he needs. Until then, he should have as a guide the wise counselor who understands this fact and has enough of a database to share.

Space for Discernment

When referring to "space" for discernment, we can talk about physical space for meeting or emotional/spiritual space for thinking. The good mentor provides both. He will listen and get to know you in these spaces. And he will provide the type of spaces that allow you to think through the numerous questions and concerns, celebrations and frustrations that crop up in the course of your vocational path.

Some of the greatest moments of clarity I have experienced have come from the probing questions and insightful observations that my mentors have presented to me. These dialogues were helpful because they were the spaces I needed to "hear myself." Countless conversations with Dr. M. Shawn Copeland affirmed my ministry in the academy. Without physical and emotional/spiritual space, I may not have arrived at some things as quickly and as clearly—or at all. These are spaces of discernment.

Such conversations and moments with a wise mentor will challenge you. They will make you think about the crises you feel led to resolve. They provide you with an opportunity to think through how your gifts can respond to ministry problems. They will make you think about the preparation you need to be equipped for this ministry and about the partners and resources you have available to complete the task. These spaces and "aha moments" will help you hear God a little bit better.

Advocacy

The mentor also has a responsibility to you in the form of advocacy. For the most part, the mentor has access to spaces where the apprentice does not. Years of experience have provided the mentor with denominational responsibilities, clergy relationships and networks, and duties that are not a part of the new minister's portfolio. She can do her best, however, to create the types of opportunities for you to acquire these things. I do not mean to suggest that a mentor should place the apprentice in a position she has not earned or assign a task she is not equipped to complete. For example, students often ask me to produce letters of recommendation for graduate school programs or ordination proceedings. If I am a person's mentor, I must know that person's qualifications. I cannot write a glowing recommendation to a graduate school for a person who shows no real potential for success at the graduate school level. The same applies for the ministry mentor's advocacy.

The mentor therefore has to know the apprentice before consenting to be her advocate. She can use this knowledge to create space for the apprentice to learn and develop. It is no coincidence that ministers recommend certain people when churches invite preachers to fill their pulpits. Ministry mentors often know which church will receive a certain person better than another. Or a mentor may float an apprentice's name to do a workshop because that person's gifts suggest that she functions better in that setting.

Advocacy may not be for a preaching or teaching engagement. Some mentors are discerning enough to link an apprentice with a broader network of people that is doing a ministry that fits their protégé. An apprentice then has an opportunity to see that she is not alone, to share resources, and to share in new conversations with new partners in ministry. All of these things stem from a discerning mentor's concern for the apprentice as a person and for her ministry.

We cannot deny reality when it comes to advocacy. There *is* a network of good ole boys and "gals." Even God's people will select from their short list of friends, protégés, and colleagues. This is not necessarily a bad thing. Some people do abuse this relationship, but my hope is that mentors are advocates with integrity.

Prayer

The words of the gospel song echo in our ears on this matter: "Somebody prayed for me, had me on her mind. . . . Took the time to pray for me." Prayer is that essential practice in our faith that encourages us to seek God's guidance for our lives. The mentor who prays for you will believe in seeking God's guidance to counsel you. I remember that Pastor Thornhill ended every meeting he had with me with a moment of prayer. Those prayers reminded me of his concern for me and of my relationship with God. Prayer is an important practice that keeps us in communication with the God who called us.

What Is Your Duty?

You have some responsibilities in this mentoring relationship. Your investment in the time spent with your mentor will help create the opportunity for both of you to grow. You have as much to teach the mentor as your mentor has to share with you. Although the lessons are different, they are nevertheless valuable. Depending on the differences in age, perspective, and experiences, you may give your ministry mentor new ideas and resources to work with in ministry. To be sure, you must be willing to do your part.

Time

Just as it is essential for the ministry mentor to make time for you, you must make time for your mentor. A relationship can blossom with the investment of time and die without it. Be available to meet with your ministry mentor and prepare to work around his schedule. We all have lives—busy lives—so the mentor will not always be accessible. Your commitment to serious conversation can make the time that you do have meaningful. Do not abuse the time—your mentor may be sharing his time with other protégés.

Patience and Understanding

Patience and understanding are important qualities for ministry protégés. While ministry mentors have a rich database to share, they do not know everything. And not every idea they have will fit the protégé's ministry context. Moreover, while being in ministry for many years has benefits, it also has some disadvantages. Ministers may fall into the comfortable pace of repetition. Our déjà vu–like experiences may dull our insights. And we may limit our circle of contacts to people who have similar ministry ideas and practices. We may unintentionally limit our world of influences to fit our comfort level. Ministry protégés may therefore challenge their mentors to broaden their ideas.

Harry Emerson Fosdick, the late great preacher of the Riverside Church in New York, shared the story of his counsel to noted theologian Reinhold Niebuhr. Both men were known for their impatience with proponents of fundamentalist Christian theology. But Niebuhr believed that Fosdick did not offer enough in his attack against the Fundamentalists. The two came face-to-face for some occasion or another. And in a brief, private conversation between the two, Fosdick told Niebuhr that he (Fosdick) was fighting the battle of his time. Fosdick encouraged Niebuhr to fight the battle of Niebuhr's time. It should be our hope that ministry mentors will help equip us for the battles of our time.

Space for Discernment and Openness

As important as it is for the ministry mentor to create spaces for discernment, you can do the same for yourself. Making time and space available to think through the conversations and the heavy lifting of spiritual discernment is important. You may recognize that God is not leading you to the place where you thought you would do ministry. But know that having a space for the Spirit to do God's work in you will produce magnificent results. In the Acts of the Apostles, we see the results of a ministry mentor's guidance with his protégés (see Acts 2). Jesus worked with the disciples for a few years, teaching and counseling. Once the disciples had time to reflect on his teaching, the Spirit grabbed hold of them. Pentecost happened!

Prayer

Your upper room experience can happen, and prayer can advance that possibility. Finding time for prayer makes time with God a key component in the discernment process. Your willingness to invest in prayer displays your attempt to make God a priority in your journey.

It is only through their faithfulness to authentic and meaningful dialogue and sharing that both individuals in the mentoring relationship receive the blessing of growth in their journey together. Several passages of Scripture show us the importance of the ministry mentor. For example, Deborah's counsel to Barak made it possible for Israel to claim victory (Judges 4–5). Naomi, Ruth's ministry mentor, provided Ruth with guidance, and Ruth's devotion to Naomi's wisdom is noteworthy (Ruth 1–4). The story of Elijah and Elisha also shows us how rich the mentoring relationship can be (2 Kings 2). To be sure, these stories also teach us that mentoring relationships last only for a season. We must make the most of them to receive our "double portion" of ministry power and clarity. God has blessed us with people who have walked where God has placed them to do God's work. We all can benefit from these people and their experiences. They help us to move beyond a mere reliance on our charisma and charm.

With this knowledge in hand, I ask that you recognize the people who have yet to take steps beyond their ministry call. Carefully consider how you can become a mentor, just as you are being mentored now.

Questions TO CONSIDER

1. Who are the mentor candidates in your life? What qualifies them as candidates?

2. How do you use the time that you spend with your current mentor(s)?

3. What are some of the lessons that you have learned from your mentor(s)?

4. How do you apply this wisdom in your ministry?

NOTE

1. The Fund for Theological Education sponsored a mentoring workshop for its alumni. The focus of the session included strategies for nurturing the voices of the next generation of leaders in the academy and the church. I attended the workshop in June 2009, receiving much to think about in my own mentoring ministry.

CHAPTER 3

Where Charisma Will Not Take You

Comic books were one of my favorite genres for reading as a child. The classic story of good triumphing over evil always captured me. The colorful superheroes, costumes, and personalities jumped off the pages into my imagination. For each lead comic book character, the writer would at some point provide an origin narrative. That narrative pointed to the special moment when the hero became a paragon of justice. To be sure, there was something special about these heroes already. The brains, instincts, courage, and sense of duty were resident in the moral fabric of their being. A "call" or beckoning, though, would bring out their purpose.

Look at the Spider-Man character, for example. A radioactive spider bite amplified what was already in him. Peter Parker, Spider-Man's alter ego, was already a budding scientist with a bright mind and sensitivity to people's needs. The event that gave him his spider powers sealed his fate to a "higher calling." He became Spider-Man and learned to respect that "with great power comes great responsibility." Or as Jesus makes clear, to whom much is given, much is required (Luke 12:48).

In some cases, a mentor/authority figure taps the potential hero for service. The Marvel Comics character Professor Xavier identifies the gifted mutants (X-Men) in the world and invites them to make it a better place. Obi-Wan Kenobi is a clarion voice for Luke Skywalker. In other cases, the potential hero sees a need and rushes in to help save the day. The call to duty is a common theme. Our famous comic book heroes, now finding celebrity in movie theaters across the world, always seek to make the world a better place through servant leadership. They respond to the call to service, employing their gifts and abilities. Can we say the same for the vocational development of the minister? Most people may not want to compare their call to that of a comic book character, but in this case, life imitates art. While the minister is not a superhuman, the role and responsibilities sometimes require near superhuman ability. But the minister cannot make it on ability alone.

Charisma and the Minister

Charisma is an important part of your vocational journey. What is charisma? Paul's use of the word *gift* in 1 Corinthians 12 is a form of the Greek word *charisma*—free gift. God endows each person with a personality package that is free to grow in response to the nurture, love, and environment provided for that person. In other words, something in you responds to life and love (or the lack of love), influencing the path you take. That package is a part of your charisma. Paul's conversation about the source of the gifts is clear: God gives the gifts. Our challenge is to figure out what to do with them.

Paul distinguishes that the gifts are for the community. In the Corinthian community, speaking in tongues was a popular gift. Everybody wanted to have that gift! In 1 Corinthians 12–14, Paul attempts to move his readers at Corinth away from using their gifts as a selfish, pietistic, attention grab. He shares with them the value of the diverse body of gifts that God has made available. Every person has an assignment in ministry, and both assignments and gifts differ from person to person according to God's distribution of them.

We all bring to ministry something unique to our person, a gift of grace that God invested in us. The call from God affirms this and invites us to use our gift in service to others. God requests that we use our gifts and person (whole self) to transform the world. Yet this is only one side of the story. The initial investment of charisma is just that. We come to ministry with gifts and skills that require some cultivating and nurture. To return to the comic books, the hero does not become a hero overnight. He or she needs to prepare. Just as most superheroes remain human (and have a "fatal flaw" or weakness), even more does the minister remain very much human and very much flawed. Like Superman, every person has a kryptonite.

The minister needs some time to adjust, to learn how to use new abilities, and to develop complementary tools. The hero has to get the right look for his costume and persona. A hero has to master his powers. A mentor may help a minister adjust and adapt to ministry leadership. Such was the case with Joshua. He had guidance from Moses. That experience helped Joshua step in to Moses' ministry leadership position. Or the hero may work out the details of his ability on his own, but he realizes that the initial package will not provide for him everything he needs to fight the villains. He needs time to harness his ability.

As a new minister, you may find yourself in this position. You have gifts and abilities, the natural equipment for ministry. But God's call for your life requires that you think through and prepare yourself for the ministry God places before you. Without spending this time preparing, you risk selling yourself short—cheapening your ministry. The minister who aims at acquiring a title and sitting in the reserved section that is the pulpit seeks no more than a badge of honor. The preacher who looks to live off natural ability or charismatic gifts without intentional preparation only robs the people of the blessed power that could flow through her life. Charisma is an influential part of our ministry that is only *a part* of the work that God does in us for ministry. The power of personality, native vocal gifts, resident counseling instincts, and charm and good looks can go only so far in this journey. Those things can move people, but you want to provide them with more.

Moving from a reliance on innate gifts to living into the distinct call from God is necessary. Integrity requires that you give your all to investing in preparation. It is no coincidence that Paul tells Timothy to stir up the gifts within him and to study to show himself approved by God (see 2 Timothy 1:6; 2:15).

As compelling and inspiring as your natural gifts may be to people, God expects more from you.

Tools for Ministry Discernment

Before moving too quickly to practice ministry as a "professional," taking a gifts and/or personality assessment is a wise step. Numerous evaluation tools are available for helping people to think intentionally about their gifts, and some denominations provide career counseling to aid ministers in their vocational journeys.

At the seminary where I teach, we work with the Center for Career Development and Ministry to facilitate vocational discernment. Our seminary requires a course for ministry formation. In the course, seminarians take personality assessments and fill out ministry skills inventories.[1] This course is part of our attempt to help our community listen to what God is saying about vocation. Another component of the course is a one-on-one session with a counselor who aids each seminarian in interpreting the assessment results. This conversation allows seminarians to think in more detail about what God has placed in them. Students who have taken the course come out of it with a sense of discovery. They are able to see some of the connections between their personalities and their ministry gifts. The person who is an extrovert may enjoy public appearances, kissing babies, and shaking hands much more than the introverted person. The ministry introvert may draw more energy and enjoyment from solitary moments of study and reflection or from a one-on-one visit in hospitals or homes.

An example of an assessment instrument can give us a better sense of how such instruments are used. Consider the many skills and gifts you bring to ministry. How many times have you sat down and thought about them? Most of us don't reflect on the skills and gifts that go into accomplishing our ministry work. This sample questionnaire can help us identify some strengths and growing edges early in the process:

Circle the feeling or activity that best reflects how you feel about the skill or activity.

Advising

Providing guidance and counsel.

Referring people to others.

Administration

Leading people, doing managerial tasks.

Carrying out directions from senior staff.

Schedule

Prefer a 9 to 5 schedule.

Prefer to make my own schedule.

Work-Related Activity

Desk job, high-volume reports and paperwork.

People-focused, highly interactive.

Preaching

Enjoy sermon preparation and preaching.

Would prefer a less visible role.

Christian Education

Enjoy lesson plans and presentation.

Curriculum and teaching are not my strength.

Pastoral Counseling

Prefer spiritual guidance, listening, and empathy.

Prefer less emotional involvement.

Research and Writing

Critical reading, reflection, and reporting.

Prefer these tasks only when necessary.

Travel

Business trips or mission field.

I am a homebody.

Education

Advanced studies, professional/vocational education.

School is not for me.

As simple as the responses to these skill sets and preferences may seem, they may help you identify your passion areas and areas of expertise. And you may want to take assessments at various stages in your professional life as you and your call evolve. Taking the time to reflect on the skills you acquire and your changing interests in certain ministry tasks is important.

Other resources and people are available to help you with your search for authenticity in ministry. If you are in college or you work in a company with a human resources department, you may be able to access "discernment tools." I visited the Career Resource Center on campus more than a few times during my days in graduate school. The staff provided me with resources for composing a résumé and offered skills assessment workshops. Your company may have a human resources office that has personality assessment or skills evaluation programs. Taking advantage of these opportunities will equip you for leadership where you are and where you are going.

A brief word about assessment tools is in order. Mental health professionals, in some people's view, offer only "human wisdom." Persons who are critical of mental health professions often equate going to see a counselor, psychiatrist, or psychologist with a confession of mental instability. In some cases, however, the opposite may be the truth. Not going to see a mental health professional when needed may lead to bigger emotional and physiological problems. Praying down the help we need is an important part of our Christian faith practices. And believing that God can work through the minds and hearts of people with educational preparation in mental health can demonstrate faith as well. Many Christian—and non-Christian—counselors display a respect for a person's faith. They do not want to contradict a person's faith; they want people to flourish in life within a framework that affirms those faith practices. Finding the right mental health practitioner when needed is the real task. Referrals from primary care physicians and pastoral leaders/clergy members can help you find that person.

A Word about Vocational Fit[2]

One of the biggest challenges in ministry is determining where you fit. You may be asking questions like these: Should I be in a rural or urban congregation? What would I do with a PhD? Can I use my previous professional expertise? What am I supposed to do? Where am I supposed to serve? How do I get to that point?

Consider the tools, resources, and resource people I mentioned above. They offer a service of discernment that our gifts cannot reveal to us as quickly and as clearly as we would like. They help us hear God in a way that can shed light on our journey. They help us identify some of the God-given gifts and personality traits that are meant for our ministries. Utilizing these resources can be a part of the self-discovery that makes us ready for service. Does this mean that people who do not use these tools will be unsuccessful? Of course not. I am, however, advocating for the prepared minister who embraces the benefits of these discernment tools. I found these tools useful for my journey. My decision to become a seminary professor was the product of sustained reflection and prayerful conversations with God. The opportunity to wrestle with our call to ministry and learn more about ourselves is a blessing.

To Thine Self Be True

Knowing what you are called to do is a prerequisite for determining a good place to do ministry. After you send in an application for a ministry position, the waiting can produce some good results. Waiting to hear from job search committees can prompt moments to reflect on vocational choices. The time between sending one's application materials in to hearing from the search committee can often feel like an eternity. What should you do with that time? Continue to figure out what God is calling you to do.

Calls and job searches provide you opportunities to reflect on what it means to be authentic—the real you. The time-consuming preparation of application materials can serve as an occasion for you to reexamine your direction in life. You may ask multiple times in your life "What am I being called to do?" because you have abilities and qualities that work well in multiple settings. I, for example, have traits suited for both academia and congregational life. The part of me that enjoys and is equipped to do research, writing, and teaching can find its home in the academy and the church. The product of those skills and passions are a celebrated part of the academic environment. But those same attributes are a good fit in the church as well. Researching, reflecting, and presenting-preaching-teaching match a leadership position in the church. (You have to have something to preach for people to appreciate your preaching.) The "pastoral side" of me that wants people to be engaged in conversations and activities that enhance their personhood can function in both settings. I want to mentor, instruct, celebrate with, and console as a part of my duties. I want to identify potential in a person and develop leadership. These qualities are compatible with the environments where I see myself serving.

You may be thinking, *You could have your cake and eat it too.* Be a pastor and a . . . You would not be the first person to express this sentiment. In 2006 I asked a former classmate about his success in the academic job market after a professional conference. He told me that he had no leads and that he admired my situation. What he meant by that was that if I could not find an academic post, I could always serve a church. But for me, it is not about just any position. The question is, which setting will allow me to be me? Here is where my idealism seeps through the pages of this text. I do not just want a job. I want to touch lives with the work I do. I know, I am asking for a lot—including poverty perhaps. I can hear you questioning my reasoning: *Do you enjoy being a seminary professor?* Yes. This vocation matches the gifts that God gave me. Is that what God called and equipped me to do? Yes. Could I be a local church pastor who encourages the positive changes that take place in a person's life? Yes. Is that what God called and equipped me to do? Not yet, or maybe not at all. Who knows? Can I do both at the same time? I probably cannot do both well, not if I want to live past the age of forty-five and do a decent job for both communities. Would I be happy with either position? Sure. My vocation is to be authentic—the real me—by making use of who I am and what I have (i.e., personality, education, skills, etc.) in whatever work I am led to do. A job with a salary and benefits is a bonus.

Taking Our Time in Ministry

The apostle Paul's story gives us a better sense of the need for discernment and preparation. Upon his conversion (Acts 9), he was blind and led into Damascus where the Lord prepared Ananias to affirm this conversion experience. Ananias helped Paul (who was then Saul), regain his sight and receive the filling of the Spirit. Saul was then baptized. And verse 19 stands out to me: "After taking some food, he regained his strength. For several days he was with the disciples in Damascus."

Before Paul ran out and preached, he was in conversation with and, more than likely, learning from those disciples in Damascus. To be sure, one should not discount the fact that he was already a learned Torah scholar. But he did not get up right away and start a church. Consider verse 22 as a logical follow-up to verse 19: "Saul *became* increasingly more powerful and confounded the Jews who lived in Damascus by proving that Jesus was the Messiah" (emphasis added). May God empower all of us to have an impact on the world similar to that of Paul's ministry.

In the late '90s, I went to see the film *Everest* in an IMAX theater. That movie gives me one last analogy for this chapter. The filmmakers captured the story of several climbers who scaled Mount Everest, the tallest mountain in the world. I learned a lot from watching this film, but the primary lesson dealt with the dangers of climbing in high altitudes. As the climbers ascended, the amount of oxygen became thinner. The climbers risked suffering from health complications such as hypoxia, which could lead to other problems. So to reach the apex of the mountain, the climbers needed to stop and adjust to the thin air. If climbers moved too quickly, they could succumb to a climbing-related illness. To reach the top, they needed to stop and adjust to the environment before climbing higher. Attempting to reach the top too quickly endangered the mission.

To put this in perspective for ministers, we need to consider an important idea about physical ability and internal drive. The climbers' innate abilities and equipment could help them march up the mountain. Nothing stopped their feet from moving forward or quenched their desire to climb higher. But the laws of nature made sure they knew that the journey took patience and perseverance, not just charisma (personality) and ability.

What can we learn from this illustration? First, conditioning and preparation are needed before climbing a mountain or ascending the heights of high-profile ministry. Second, we need to take time to climb to the "top." Success that comes too soon may be hazardous to the health of the minister and the congregation/

people. There is a celebrity culture in ministry, and unfortunately some people want to mimic these "stars" and rise quickly for a higher profile or status in ministry. Some people believe they are fit to pastor a church the day after God calls them. While that may be the case, the experiences of many people in ministry show the need for a season of discernment and preparation. If the goal is the apex of the mountain, we need to allow ourselves time to adjust to the heights that God allows us to reach. Moving too quickly may endanger our God-given mission.

What God calls you to do will be there waiting for you in God's time. Your ministry has the potential to change lives in wonderful ways. Give God your all by taking advantage of the resources available to empower you. These will only help you along the way. They are the tools for ministry self-discovery, providing what charisma alone does not reveal instantly. And many of the tools for this purpose reside in the formal theological education curriculum.

Next Steps

- Find a resource center that offers and assesses a personality and skills evaluation. This could be as close as the career center on your campus or human resource office at your place of employment. The assessment may include a spiritual gifts inventory. Be sure to talk with someone who knows how to interpret the results.

- Talk with friends or family members who know you well. Ask them for an honest take on some of your skills and personality traits. Encourage them to be specific. For example, "You worked well with people when you led those meetings. Encouraging ideas and giving leadership to projects seems to energize you."

- Find a mentor if you have not done so already. If you already have a mentor or mentors, continue the conversation with them and with your pastor. These people are a part of the resource team that can shed light on your "fit" in ministry. Mentors can also help you think through your next steps.

• Think through what the preparation steps are for your journey, and be sure to continue to pray for guidance.

Questions TO CONSIDER

1. What are the gifts that you bring to ministry? Write them on a piece of paper or type them on your computer.

2. How do your gifts match the call that you identified?

3. What blogs, websites, and/or Facebook groups can you subscribe to, visit, or join to learn about your desired ministry work?

4. With whom can you talk to get clarity about ministry opportunities that match your gifts?

NOTES

1. See www.ccdmin.org. Examples of these assessment instruments include the Strong Interest Inventory, the Myers-Briggs Type Indicator (MBTI), and the Emotional Quotient Inventory (EQ-i). Your local church may also offer spiritual gifts assessments. All of these instruments, if used properly, can help you in the discernment process.

2. A portion of this text was taken from my post on the Fund for Theological Education "Nurturing the Next Generation of Scholars" doctoral blog, "The Search for Authenticity—and a Job," http://www.fteleaders.org/blog/entry/the-search-for-authenticityand-a-job/.

CHAPTER 4

The Unwritten Rules of Ministry

In many ways, ministry is no different from most professions. But clergy are bound to a higher calling and ethical approach in their professional affairs. Denominational bodies may have a code of ethics and policies to influence an understanding of ministerial conduct. The American Baptist Churches USA is a perfect example. Their national Ministers Council created a code of ethics that is a part of the ordination process. Ordination candidates sign this statement to affirm that they will be accountable to and will maintain a moral standard appropriate for their ministerial duties. Signing the statement is optional, because the local church ordains in the Baptist tradition, not the national convention, but it reflects the minister's commitment and responsibility to a local church and a larger professional community. Other denominations have similar documents that stress a certain topic such as financial or sexual integrity. While these documents are important for reminding ministers of these moral and spiritual issues, they are only binding to the extent that the body that produces them has sanctioning authority. One finds, then, that ministry functions with many unwritten rules.

Unwritten Rules

Many prevailing notions about ministry etiquette and practices in local congregations and in regional judicatories never find their home in document form. In some settings where denominational guidelines have no real influence, these may be the most important rules to know. The congregation and senior pastor often have clear expectations about how a preacher (or newly licensed minister) should function on Sunday morning and the rest of the week. As a new minister, you should at least have a sense of what those expectations entail. You are more likely to avoid the pitfall of hurt feelings or embarrassment if you are aware of some of these unwritten rules of ministry. They include, but are not limited to, the ministerial title, participation in the worship experience, attire, preaching engagements, sermon development and delivery, and ministry ambitions.

What Should They Call Me?

For many new ministers, the clergy title is an important topic of consideration. A change in title is meaningful to new ministers for several reasons. Congregations are often eager to recognize a new minister's change in status, and new ministers may want others to acknowledge the call they experience. The title is a formal way of doing that. This can be a fragile situation. The congregation that called you by your first name yesterday now needs a title before your name. This may create a measure of distance where there had been familiarity and intimacy, or it may foster respect and honor where there had been a tendency to underestimate and take for granted.

Ego and insecurities also factor into this equation for the new minister. I remember walking around introducing myself as Minister Bond as if "minister" was the first name on my birth certificate. I was eager to let the world know in posturing rather than in service that God had called me. Our insecurities promote this behavior. Many of us believe that we are being insulted if someone does not acknowledge our achievements and positions. While some people may not respect us, our title is not the source of our purpose and identity. If you are reading this book, you can probably say with assurance, "I am called and commissioned by God—with or without a title." Navigating this unwritten policy is important for maintaining your personal sense of self and ministry integrity.

Where Do I Sit?

One of the other exciting transitions for the new minister comes by way of the change in assigned seating during the worship experience. In many congregations, the minister sits in the pulpit to lead the worship experience. The pulpit, in many a preacher's mind and often in the congregational perspective, is a symbol of one's leadership status in the church. For good or for ill, this space is home for much of what the minister does on Sunday morning. And some new ministers see it as a sign of an elevated church leadership position. It is unfortunate when the acquiring of a title and a new assigned seat in the sanctuary becomes the crowning moment for the new preacher.

I speak from experience on this matter. As a young Baptist preacher, I thought I had arrived the first time I sat in the pulpit. Everybody in the house could see that I was a preacher. *Wow, I'm big-time!* I thought. I would later learn the real meaning of the pulpit. That sacred desk and the space that it occupies are places of service. Young ministers' egos, however, attempt to redefine their importance. Ministers are leaders in worship, and their conduct sets an example for the seriousness of the activity. A desire for attention and affirmation can make a minister in the pulpit a source of entertainment. It can redirect worship, making the minister—not God—its focus. How should the minister, then, approach the subject of station in worship?

Luke 14:7-11 is a fitting summary for this matter. In this account, Jesus has a meal at the home of a "leading" Pharisee one Sabbath. His discerning nature keys in on a number of the other guests who are choosing seats at the finer stations of the table, and he instructs the group with a parable. He tells them that if someone invites you to a wedding feast, do not rush to sit at the most prestigious place at the table. Someone "more distinguished" than you may be among the guests who attend. The host may then have to ask you to move, embarrassing you in front of the rest of the guests. Instead, enter the feast humbly. Be careful about broadcasting your status, and choose your seat with this in mind. The host may then see you and invite you to move up to a more prestigious place at the table. Jesus' lesson is simple: people who make themselves great will be humbled, and humble people will be made great. Greatness does not need to advertise itself with a seat in the pulpit. Be great and other people will find you and extend honor to you. And as Jesus taught his disciples, the greatest among us are those who choose to be servants of all (Mark 10:44). I fear that some of us choose popularity over greatness.

What Should I Do?

Every pastor has a different understanding about the role of ministers in worship. In some congregations, laypeople carry out duties in the worship experience. A layperson may read the Scripture or lead worship. The pastor may, however, expect ministers—or ministerial associates—to perform these responsibilities. A pastor, therefore, may or may not invite you into the pulpit as a new minister. Some larger churches have several associate ministers and few seats in the pulpit. The pastor may designate a front pew where the associates sit in worship. In some settings, the new minister may sit with family members and enter the pulpit only to preach a sermon or perform some other special assignment. Seeking clarity about where to sit is important so that you do not suffer an indignity over the matter. But what do you do when you are at the rostrum?

Leading Worship

Sitting and presenting before a congregation is a skill that comes with time, polish, and education. The first few times in the pulpit—for anything—are not easy. As a child, I sat in the pulpit on youth Sundays. My peers and I always had some responsibility in the order of worship. We read litanies or Scripture lessons, said prayers, or read the morning announcements. Those early occasions in the pulpit were knee-knocking events that required adjustments. First, we needed the repetition of youth Sundays to become acquainted with being in the pulpit. Regular times of responsibility helped us get used to being leaders in worship. Second, we needed to practice. The youth coordinators and our parents became drill sergeants. We learned our parts and learned them again. We were ready by Sunday morning. Third, those occasions taught us the meaning of our activity in worship, what the liturgy meant, the importance of the prayer, and many other lessons. We knew what we were doing when the moment for service arrived. (The execution of our duties without some missteps, giggles, and awkward pauses is a different story.) The leaders did not believe in making the children merely imitate them. They were concerned about nurturing our gifts and encouraging us to express them. Our leaders should push new ministers in the same way.

Pulpit Decorum

The pulpit is a focal point in the worship experience, the place from which the Word of God is proclaimed. Often centrally positioned at the front of the sanctuary, the pulpit's prominent locale reflects its significance in worship. Whenever we stand in the pulpit, all eyes are on us. The "unwritten" expectation for many parishioners is that the pulpit sets the standard for conduct and decorum in worship. Frequent movement and/or conversation in the pulpit might establish unintended ideas about behavior in worship. Excess activity may distract the congregation and create an anxious space for worship. Respect the mood of worship and honor its sanctity. Neither a mannequin nor an acrobat is appropriate in most settings. Discernment is vital for conduct in the pulpit regardless of the occasion (funeral, wedding, baptism, etc.).

Order of Worship

My first course in preaching and worship helped me develop my evolving sense of the order of worship. The course came in the first term of my first year. Dr. Miles Jerome Jones, a noted preacher and professor, was my instructor. During the semester, he walked the class through the elements of an order of worship. We talked about the call to worship and the invocation. He noted that the invocation was not the time to pray for the world or for your grandmother's broken leg. He also made us aware of the historical and biblical significance of these elements in the worship experience. Most of us marveled at how wrong we had been for most of our short ministries, and we celebrated a new freedom of knowing how creative and flexible we could be within these new definitions of ministry and worship.

In light of my experiences, I want to make a couple of suggestions. While the order of worship differs across denominational lines and from congregation to congregation, certain aspects of worship are standard. Most congregations include in the order of worship an invocation, Scripture lesson, and benediction. Knowing the do's and don't's of these moments is essential for the new minister.

Invocation. The invocation is a time of inviting God's presence into the worship experience. This prayer reminds the gathered body to welcome God among them as they enter a period of reverence. A written or extemporaneous prayer should reflect this emphasis. Consider these examples:

> Ever-present Lord, who has taught us in your Word that where your faithful gather in obedience, there you are in the midst of them: Be present, we pray of you, in this your church's worship. Grant that our praise and our prayers may be worthy of your presence. Grant that in the unity of your Son and your Holy Spirit that we may be bound together as one body in the truth of the ages. Through Jesus, we pray. Amen.[1]

> As we worship you, O God, unstop our ears, that we might hear your word. Sweep the cobwebs from our minds, that we may receive your truth. Strengthen our wills, that we may become your true disciples. And warm our hearts, that we may receive a full measure of your love. Amen.[2]

Scripture lesson. Reading the Scripture is a matter that varies with faith traditions and congregational preferences. In some places, the Scripture readings follow the Christian calendar or lectionary. The lectionary lists a set of Scriptures that correspond with the seasons (Advent, Lent, Pentecost, etc.) in the life of the church. A preacher-pastor may use these Scriptures for the morning sermon to honor the season of the Christian calendar and its theological meaning. In some settings, the pastor may ask the ministerial worship leader to select a Scripture or Scriptures. In this case, you should ask the morning preacher for the sermon text and preferred translation or version. The preacher may read it again. It does not hurt for the people to hear the Scripture presented more than once. Consider reading the text from a version or translation that the congregation recognizes unless asked otherwise. If the members use a pew Bible, become familiar with it. Reading in a clear and engaging manner is imperative. The congregation appreciates a reader who respects correct pronunciation, punctuation marks, and their ears.

Benediction. The benediction, or parting words of blessing for the congregation, finds its home at the end of most worship experiences. Some choose to use cherished Scripture passages such as Numbers 6:24-26, "The LORD bless you and keep you; the LORD make his face to shine upon you, and be gracious to you; the LORD lift up his countenance upon you, and give you peace" and 2 Corinthians 13:14, "The grace of the Lord Jesus Christ, and the love of God, and the communion of the Holy Ghost, be with you all. Amen." The more you grow, the more you may feel led to write your own benedictions. But it is key that the function of that portion of worship never changes: sending the people out with a blessing.

I remember a catchy phrase from a college classmate that provides a final thought about leading portions of the order of worship. Kimberly Moss was the student director of the University of Memphis gospel choir. She would present the choir at various churches and give words of appreciation at other events. Before her comments, she would sometimes state that she would try to attend to three B's: Be good, Be brief, Be gone. Whatever the assignment, this motto is a solid rule to follow. Be careful about suggesting, believing, and/or stating that the Spirit is leading you to do something the pastor has not requested. If the pastor asks you to read the Scripture, please be discerning before you take seven minutes to share a personal testimony. This may not endear you to the pastor or the people. If you are not sure, ask the pastor, because the pastor is the leader of the congregation.

Dressing for Success

The minister's dress may be a trickier subject for some than it is for others. Some churches expect their ministers to be vested in traditional clergy robes, with ordained ministers adding a stole that represents the liturgical season (e.g., blue for Advent, purple for Lent, green for Common Time) or other religious or cultural symbols. In other congregations, clergy attire is more corporate contemporary, with male and female clergy wearing tailored business suits. In still other church traditions, the culture is casual, and ministers set the tone with open collars, casual slacks, and relaxed fabrics. Ministers who serve in contexts outside the parish setting may choose attire that emphasizes or downplays their clergy identity as appropriate. For example, chaplains may opt for a traditional clergy shirt and collar so that they are easily identified in the hospital corridors or among the uniforms of first responders. A minister whose call is to theological education may dress up, or down, as their academic institutions require.

Essentially, your ministry context will shape the standards for ministerial attire. As a new minister, you can probably discover what is acceptable and expected in your setting by looking at what your pastor and associate ministers wear. If all the other clergy at your church wear robes, you may assume you are expected to do the same. If you are new to your setting, keep your eyes open—and when in doubt, ask someone.

The issue of appropriate clergy garb is a sensitive one for female ministers in many settings. A man is probably safe in choosing a dress shirt, suit, and tie, with a clergy robe in the car or closet as a backup. A woman's choice may vary dramatically from one setting to another. She may be accustomed to wearing a nice pantsuit or a lovely sundress at her home church, but when preaching elsewhere, the unwritten rules may require any woman in the pulpit to wear a skirt of a certain length (with stockings) and sleeves that cover her shoulders.

Dress is an important subject, because ministry can mimic society. Ministers may follow changes in fashion. Many Protestant clergy borrow from other Christian traditions to fit a certain look. One of my Baptist seminary classmates purchased a cassock. I asked why he chose that instead of a "traditional" clergy robe. His response was simple: "This fits my look. I am a young man; robes are for the older generation." Years of observation led me to believe that his concern was style. At that time, one found cassocks most often in non-Protestant or "high church" traditions. The 1990s saw more Protestants donning such attire. And after all, there is no universal uniform for clergy. The "uniform" has been a cultural construction.

In the early days of the church until the present, cultural and religious ideas about clergy attire have shifted. For example, some early church leaders merely encouraged ministers to wear something clean! By the third century clergy wore either all white or all black clothing. Some leaders wanted ministers to distinguish themselves by their learning, not their dress. One author notes that there is no real record of early church leaders being concerned about appropriate clergy attire. The minister's clothing did not differ from the laity.[3] As time passed, clergy apparel modeled academic regalia. (We still see this kind of robe in many pulpits today.) In the United States, specifically, ministers in the twentieth century began to look more like Wall Street executives. They fashioned their garb after CEOs and even began to see themselves as chief executives of their congregations. In the twenty-first century, pastors in the emergent church and even some seeker-focused megachurches are dressing more informally yet, in polo shirts and khakis or even blue jeans.

Regardless of the reason for the changes, dress does not outweigh duty. I hope that our concerns for style and apparel do not distract us from sincere ministry. And we may always have the assurance that, despite the unwritten rules and unspoken (or spoken!) expectations of God's people, God looks not on the outward appearance but at our hearts (1 Samuel 16:7).

Sunday Is Coming—What Do I Say?

For many who respond to the call to ministry, the first sermon is toughest. (In some instances, it is also the shortest!) You may never again in life experience the amount of anxiety felt when facing the prospect of delivering your first sermon. But the Sunday will come when it is time to give evidence of your gifts and calling. My Old Testament professor, Dr. Jerome Clayton Ross, would end each class by saying, "Sunday's coming—got to preach!"

Depending on the congregation and/or denomination, procedure compels new ministers to offer a "trial," or initial, sermon before the church. What do you say? How do you say it? The new preacher's anxiety is natural. The unwritten rule is that you should have seen enough preachers and heard enough sermons to put one together on your own. Closely related to that rule is that the new minister should not preach a long sermon. I do believe that a good sermon model can help you navigate these unwritten rules.

A helpful yet simple model comes from a writing course I took during my undergraduate days. Dr. Mary Battle teaches persuasive writing at the University of Memphis. Her course was one of the most enlightening and informative classes I took at that school. She impressed upon me the importance of making a convincing case to an audience. Public speakers and writers have little time with their audiences, so they must determine how best to get their message across to their listeners in the time or space allotted. That is the task of the preacher every Sunday. We have a short time to make a case for Christlike service to the community or to encourage our listeners to reorient their life to divine expectations. Effectiveness lies in the Holy Spirit's activity in the process, but we must give the Spirit something with which to work. Dr. Battle's model for the writing course can help us do it.

I preface the rest of this information by stating that I am not a preaching professor (and I do not play one in the movies). This information is more of an entrance into a conversation about the craft of preaching. I offer this for people who have not had the benefit of a preaching course or preaching manual. This is not a substitute for prayer, research, and critical conversations with your pastor and colleagues about the sermon's content. I am a firm believer that one does not have to develop the sermon in isolation. We all can benefit from conversations with accountability partners and from dialogue with thinkers who know more than we know.

Having made such a disclaimer, let me paraphrase and simplify Dr. Battle's teaching, which describes a structure for persuasive writing—and preaching—as being comprised of four components. The first is your main idea, expressed plainly in what I describe as a sermon capsule. This is your first sentence, which contains the central thrust of the sermon; it expresses your main idea. Ultimately you may create a sermon that has three or more points, depending primarily on the research that you complete. However, you should be able to capture the key idea, the core message, by answering this simple question: What is the point of your sermon? In many instances, it will be a single powerful sentence, clear and to the point. For example, the Luke text cited on page 38 encourages us to be humble. A good sentence capsule will describe true humility in action.

The second component of persuasive writing and preaching is termed the *proponent position*. This is your "for" argument, in which you make your case in positive terms. In the example from Luke's Gospel, you define and promote "true humility" by exploring its benefits to the individual, to the community, and even to the world. And in a gospel sermon, the proponent position will probably draw strongly on biblical examples and apply the argument in the context of our relationships with God as well as with other people.

The *contrary position* is the third component of persuasive communication. In this stage of your sermon, you consider the opposing side of your argument. It is not that you are arguing against yourself, but it does no good to pretend that a contrary perspective does not exist. By acknowledging the opposing viewpoint and reviewing the case it makes, you demonstrate respect for others' opinions as well as your confidence in your own argument. You do not need to back down or dodge your "opponent" because the gospel message you bring will stand on its own merits. So, again connecting with the humility example from Luke, you might talk about the risks of being humble—and why some may resist practicing humility over pride and self-preservation or promotion.

The final component of this four-part method from Dr. Battle is the *call to action*. After launching your message from your main point in a microcosmic sentence and exploring both the positive position and the contrary one, you return full circle, presuming that you have persuaded your listeners to the main idea. Now, what should the listener do with the information you share? How should your audience proceed after hearing the sermon? You may find your call to action in the scriptural text, or you may extract it from the biblical narrative of Jesus' life. You may find that the call emerges when you apply the biblical principle to matters of social injustice in your community or to personal tragedies or crises in your congregation. Luke's text challenges us to think not only about the people at the table; true humility calls us to also consider how we define status and who may be missing from the table. The successfully persuasive sermon leaves us with a challenge to do something with what we have heard from the preacher. This call should be clear and achievable. You want the congregation to leave the sanctuary saying, "I can do that. I can make that kind of change."

What Will They Pay Me?

It may seem premature to consider the question of payment for preaching. Many new ministers are just grateful for the opportunity to stand in the pulpit and are humbled by the privilege of sharing God's Word. Sooner or later, however, the sensitive subject of the preacher's honorarium will become relevant. The honorarium is that gift of appreciation that an organization or church gives for the minister's service. There is no standard dollar amount for this gift, and you will not find an honorarium fee scale included in most invitations to preach. This presents a challenge, especially for the newly called minister: Do you create your own fee scale or accept what the people give you? Let your conscience guide you. Some people who have a fee scale use their experience and education to suggest a desired amount. Other people feel that whatever a congregation gives them is a blessing of grace and mercy. If you are curious about these practices, ask an experienced elder.

Will They Know My Name?

Ambition in ministry is nothing new but is often unmentionable. Most people, regardless of their vocation, will eventually seek promotion and look to climb the career ladder. Ministry is often no different. Promotion generally means a higher salary and a greater measure of job security. It may entail greater respect from one's peers and additional opportunities for personal and professional development. How exactly you define promotion in ministry depends on your ambitions. Do you aspire to the stature and visibility of the celebrity minister, either at the local or national level? Do you connect that aspiration to the impact and influence of the gospel ministry? Or is it more about an improved standard of living and social notoriety?

Even among those who do not have any ambition to become the next T. D. Jakes or Joel Osteen, there is almost inevitably a time when pastoral leaders define success by the number of members on the church roll or the average attendance on Sunday mornings.

In other ministry contexts, the numbers game may take a different form—the number of preaching engagements in a year, the number of conversions at a revival, the number of donors to a ministry program, or the climbing numbers on the capital fund-raising campaign. For some, promotion means leaving a rural church or urban storefront to pastor a large suburban congregation. Success is a spot on the program at a national conference or denominational event, or a time slot for a television or radio broadcast.

As someone who works with emerging church leaders, I must raise the red flag of concern about "success" when ambition outruns love. A look in the mirror of the soul can reveal the purpose for our actions, the motives behind our tasks. An honest observer will admit that the recognition and attention renowned preachers receive are quite appealing. Recognition and attention, however, are not the concerns that Christ defined for ministry. The well-known and highly esteemed preacher Samuel DeWitt Proctor often told the story of hearing Clarence Jordan's lecture on the Sermon on the Mount. At the end of the lecture, a person asked Dr. Jordan how a modern, urban, successful pastor could meet the standards that Jesus called for in the sermon. Proctor celebrated Jordan's response: "Jesus did not give the sermon to modern, urban, successful pastors. He gave it to his disciples. One has to decide if one is going to be a disciple or a modern, urban, successful pastor."

I pray that God helps *you* make the right decision.

Questions TO CONSIDER

1. What unwritten rules have you identified from your ministry context?

2. What unwritten rules concern you? In what ways do they become sources of concern?

3. How do you navigate some of the unwritten rules? Who coaches you through them? What advice do you receive?

NOTES

1. Orlando L. Tibbetts, *The Minister's Handbook* (Valley Forge, PA: Judson Press, 1986), 23–24.

2. John E. Skoglund and Nancy E. Hall, *A Manual of Worship, New Edition* (Valley Forge, PA: Judson Press, 1993), 46.

3. J. K. Shryock, "The Distinctive Dress of the Clergy," *Anglican Theological Review* 25, no. 4 (October 1943): 374–88.

PART TWO

Preparing for Excellence in Ministry

CHAPTER 5

Study to Show Yourself Approved:

Three Years of Self-Discovery

Because each minister's vocational journey is unique, the question of theological education as preparation for ministry may arise early or late, before or after licensing, before or after the initial sermon. In some traditions, the question may rarely arise at all. I've chosen to place this chapter at the center of the book, not for chronological reasons (because there is no fixed or universal order for the call process) but for theological reasons. Ministers are first and foremost disciples themselves, and the core of the disciple's identity is that of being a lifelong learner.

Learning is one of the things that never ceases in ministry. There is always something on the horizon that requires reading and studying. Composing each sermon sends the preacher into the library in a search for meaning. Resources abound on bookstore and library shelves, in online journals and through Internet searches. Conferences and workshops provide the minister with an opportunity to think deeply for hours or days at a time about important ministry matters. A multitude of resources and spaces can nurture the minister as student in an ongoing way.

Making Choices

Around late August each year hundreds of thousands of people are preparing to start their first year of higher education. The anxieties and nervous energy that come with this can be overwhelming. You must download quickly a lot of new information—from the campus map to the locations of restrooms—and find your way among new faces and spaces. I would not be surprised to hear you ask, "Am I in the right place?" But your query may not be about the location of a class or office. Instead, you may be pondering the decision that led you to enroll in school. Why get a formal education? Why, moreover, apply for formal *theological* education? I have one simple answer for this: Sunday school and Bible study will not cover everything you need to know for ministry.

As suggested above, education in formal settings may happen at any stage of a minister's journey. Many of the students who attend my seminary are already licensed and ordained. Some come to seminary with years of ministry experience. Formal theological education is not a prerequisite to licensure or ordination in some congregational settings. Such practices make a conversation about ministry preparation important for this book.

An apprenticeship with a pastor and attendance at sporadic or annual conferences all aid in ministerial formation. In addition to these people and events, ministers in this age have the opportunity to avail themselves to the vast resources of theological education. The seminary has the educational structure and curricular offerings to aid ministers. Once ministers get beyond the first-day jitters, the journey through seminary can bless them richly, thereby blessing everyone they serve. Their increase in knowledge and understanding is also the people's gain. The choice should not be education or no education but what type of education you should obtain.

At least four distinct and sometimes overlapping models of ministerial education exist. For the most part, ministers are not lone rangers when it comes to learning. Some of us do not restrict our learning opportunities to personal study and Christian education at the church (i.e., Sunday school, Bible study, and vacation Bible school). Other opportunities arise—from apprenticeship with a ministry mentor to the formal curriculum of a theological school—and many of us take advantage of them. Let us consider a few examples.

Ministry Apprenticeship

The ministry apprenticeship is probably the oldest form of ministerial formation. This structured practice has the apprentice learning from a master craftsperson. From the prophets of old to current local church arrangements, new ministers connect with a "master" to "learn the ways of the 'Force.'" Ministry masters encourage their protégés by giving guidance and advice both deliberately and inadvertently. The new ministers watch and listen to figure out what they are supposed to do. Thus intentional apprenticeships are a wonderful way for new ministers to develop their craft. The "master" in this instance may not be the new minister's mentor. The mentoring relationship may grow out of this process, but it might not. For example, the ministerial associate is often an apprentice to the senior pastor, but the pastor may never see herself as a mentor to the minister. The apprenticeship may be for the sole purpose of hearing and seeing instructions about the craft of ministry. The key, I believe, is to establish expressed goals and learning outcomes. The "do as I do" model can provide only limited insight about a minister's vocation.

Conferences and Denominational Events

With the explosion of conferences and denominational events, ministers can attend a workshop or seminar monthly. Independent Christian organizations, local congregations, denominations, and individual ministers sponsor continuing education functions. These events offer ministers a space to learn, exchange ideas, and develop ministry gifts and tools.

Talks or sermons from presenters, book displays, and conference DVDs and CDs can facilitate the learning process. Hearing ideas from celebrated preachers and pastors can be an enriching experience. Scholars and other professionals may provoke thought and enlighten you on some issue or theme. You may also come home with a reading list that can stimulate you. Presenters come in both genders and with an array of styles and presentation methods that challenge their audiences to be better.

Networking is another good reason to attend conferences, since people from various locales may attend an event. Local church conferences may include sister congregations in the city or state. Regional conferences may draw people from across the state line. And national conferences may include people from the fifty states and beyond. You will have the opportunity to converse with other ministers and laypeople in this diverse audience with whom you share interests, methodology, and views.

Another, not necessarily final, reason to attend seminars and conferences is for rest and renewal. Full-time parish ministers and bivocational ministers need outlets for the aforementioned reasons and to rest. "Even God rested on the seventh day," a pastor says. Ministers need continuing education events for personal renewal. We need someone to minister to us. A conference schedule presents an occasion for rest and reflection. For this reason, many pastors negotiate continuing education into their compensation packages.

While some events are dedicated solely to continuing education, other events include denominational business. If your congregation is affiliated with a denomination, the annual meeting of the organization could have moments for both business and learning. A meeting such as this can be stressful or fulfilling—or both. The "convention," as some people call it, is the family reunion for a denomination. It may provide the benefits of a conference-like atmosphere with workshops and worship experiences. The denominational convention also handles business matters and shares information about the state of the organization. Your local congregation's involvement in denominational life may suggest how active the ministerial leader should be in its dealings. As with any family reunion, the family members enjoy one another and share in a time of meaningful fellowship (or bickering).

Conferences remain a steady part of the ministerial formation option list. One must be careful, however, to discern the relevance and usefulness of these events for one's ministry. Conferences and workshops can be expensive, with registration fees, hotel stays, and transportation quickly adding up. With the availability of web feeds and conference CDs and DVDs, it is wise to be selective when choosing a conference to attend.

Bible College

Bible college is an option for some people who choose a path in ministry. Typically Bible colleges consist of two- or four-year degree programs that have a curriculum similar to a liberal arts undergraduate program. Bible schools, however, place their emphasis on a biblical education that prepares a person for ministry. They differ from seminaries by way of their focus on undergraduate preparation; seminaries offer professional degrees in graduate education. While many Bible colleges are affiliated with accreditation agencies, they may not be the same agencies that accredit "traditional" public and private colleges and universities. Some schools associated with nongovernmental accreditation agencies do not make themselves accountable to governmental suggestions for standards in higher education. Other schools that are accredited through Christian accrediting agencies do follow governmental recommendations. The Council for Higher Education Accreditation can help you determine if a school you are considering is accredited by their organization.[1] Do your research before enrolling in any school.

Consider several other matters when researching Bible colleges. A Bible college usually provides an undergraduate degree and a focus on ministry education. Comparing these colleges with traditional liberal arts colleges may reveal that the majors are limited. There may be few, if any, majors in disciplines outside of ministry. While one may see this as a benefit, the job market may suggest otherwise. Prayer and discernment must definitely be a part of the decision-making process. The typical undergraduate may leave a liberal arts college or university with a nonsectarian education, recognized by more than a handful of employers. It will depend on the institution. Do your homework on what majors are offered and on the doctrinal stance of the school.

Some Bible colleges require entering students to sign a statement of faith. Students who sign the document state that they agree to abide by the school's faith commitment and belief system. The school may ask students to agree with their positions as a condition of their acceptance. Some people suggest that having students sign a statement of faith merely raises the students' awareness of the school's beliefs. Other people argue that it stifles intellectual curiosity and creativity. They raise a simple question: Is a student of that institution free to believe contrary notions, ask questions, or pose ideas that challenge the school's beliefs? Again, diligent research can assist you in determining your path.

Seminary, Divinity School, School of Religion/Theology

Graduate professional theological education finds a home in institutions that use one of the labels in the heading. Most of the labels describe an educational institution that focuses on preparing ministerial leaders in some capacity. For the sake of this book, we will use the generic descriptor "seminary."

The seminary education is a graduate program primarily for professional religious leaders. Historically, seminaries admitted people preparing for leadership in Christian contexts. Now people come to seminary for varied reasons. For example, a person may enter a seminary to resolve questions of faith. Another person may enter seminary as a step before a graduate program in religion (e.g., a PhD or ThD degree program). The traditional track covered ministry basics for pastoral leaders. Today's seminaries still offer introductory and advanced courses in Christian education, biblical studies, pastoral counseling, church administration, preaching and worship, church history, theology, ethics, and denominational studies to give ministers a well-rounded ministry education. The courses cover ministers' Bible interpretation and preaching tasks, counseling and teaching work, and knowledge of Christian history and ethics.

The most recognized accreditation agency for seminaries is the Association of Theological Schools in North America and Canada (ATS).[2] Schools such as Vanderbilt Divinity School, American Baptist Seminary of the West, and the Samuel DeWitt Proctor School of Theology at Virginia Union University establish their standards according to this accrediting agency's guidelines.

There are other factors to consider in choosing a seminary besides its accreditation. Recommendations often come from interested church members, pastors, and alumni. My pastor recommended the School of Theology at Virginia Union while other church members suggested other places. The final choice is yours. But consider the following things along with the recommendations you receive:

- Denominational connection (some seminaries will require signing a statement of faith)

- Scholarships and financial aid available

- Diversity (or lack of diversity) of faculty and student population

- Location (warm or cold weather, urban or rural, proximity to your home, etc.)

- Degree programs (master of divinity, master of arts, master of sacred theology, etc.)

- Class sizes and faculty-to-student ratios

- Library resources

You can use these factors to rank your seminary choices. What is your order of priority? Would you prefer a seminary of the same tradition as your own or a contrasting one? Are you able to relocate to attend seminary, or are you looking for maximum flexibility in long-distance learning? Your responses help determine which schools are a good fit for you.[3] Start your research with the schools' websites, but keep in mind that websites can be misleading. Visit schools to help with your discernment process. Conversations with current students, staff, and professors can often add clarity about your choices.

Seminaries have an understanding of their educational work and goals that shape their identities. Some see their work as preparing people for ministry in a church, while others focus more on educating people for further graduate study. A few seminaries attempt to do both well. Be attentive to some of the details. There are subtle signs that give clues about this matter. For example, look at the faculty biographies. What connections do the instructors have to local churches or denominations? Check the list of required courses. Do you see a balance between courses in practical ministry matters and theory and history? Or, does the school privilege its practical ministry courses? The emphasis of that school is congregational ministry. The opposite may be the case if the school emphasizes courses such as church history, systematic theology, ethics, and sociology of religion. That school's focus may be more inclined to developing religious scholars.

These questions will assist you when you make your checklist of potential schools. Seminary is an important step in the minister's journey. Choosing the right one is important. Once you make the choice, you will benefit from an overview of what the experience offers.

Understanding the Seminary Journey

Let us assume you have made your choice for ministry preparation—and you have opted to pursue a graduate degree in professional ministry through a seminary or school of theology. You have visited the campus and liked what you saw. The orientation went well, and your application was accepted. The semester is about to begin, and you are ready to start classes. Great! Before you begin, however, an important reminder can help you with perspective on the experience.

The aim of seminary should be for you as the minister to give yourself to the process of discernment, inquiry, critical conversation, and fellowship. While participating in this process, you will have moments that clarify your faith practices and vocational path. The course materials and/or other experiences in school should assist in revealing things to you about your ministry journey. As a Baptist, your course in Baptist polity may awaken in you a new sensitivity to the practices in your church. You may connect the dots in your experience with the things that you read and hear. From where I stand, these discoveries seem to unfold in three "aha" types of moments in my classroom:

Oh! I did not know that. You will learn information about yourself and about your religious tradition that you never knew existed.

Ah! That makes sense. The new information you receive may confirm what you thought or shed light on what you could never explain.

But what about . . . ? You need more information or see a gap in what you have learned with what you thought. You need more information to make sense of your learning. You are also asking what to do with information and/or trying to uncover knowledge to complete the previous moments (the oh and the ah).

The discovery process can be simultaneously fun, frustrating, enlightening, and confusing. But it is also a rich process, molding and shaping some of the finest ministry leaders of our time. Think about these points as a preview of the path through seminary.

Seminary Is Not Sunday School

I believe the most important thing for a person to know about seminary is that it is not an advanced Sunday school class. Some people enroll in seminary believing that it is an extension of the Sunday morning church school class. Seminary education broadens the curriculum people encounter in the church. The Sunday church school curriculum provides a primer for the devotional life of the Christian. Materials survey biblical lessons for a class that lasts about an hour. The conversations vary in intensity and depth. Questions about ministry practices and resources beyond the biblical text are unlikely to enter those conversations. In contrast, seminary education emphasizes a critical (investigative) look at Christianity. The texts focus less on the devotional life and more on the background of the Christian experience, ancient and contemporary.

Compared to many local congregations, seminary allows students to ask the questions that are off-limits in a church school class. Courses in biblical studies place the Bible in its historical and spiritual context. (Depending on the instructor of the course, the emphasis could be one or the other.) Constructive theology classes ask seminarians to think about the sources that they use to construct their faith and to ask: Who is Jesus? What does he mean for salvation? What/Who is God? Seminarians attempt to address these questions in light of conversations (through readings) with Christian thinkers from different periods. In my field, church history, seminarians learn about what happens with the church after the Bible closes. It marks time by highlighting the numerous ecumenical councils and various people and events in Christian history. To be sure, an "average" congregation does not deal with this material or provide a forum to discuss it in the detail that a semester-long course provides. Instructors in the seminary are often well versed in the discipline. Course texts are, in most cases, carefully selected to give the "bigger picture."

As mentioned above, the freedom to ask tough questions is a luxury some seminaries provide. Ministers find sanctuary within some seminary walls to look at the Christian faith critically. Tradition in the local congregation may suggest that there should be a unified theological voice (i.e., one "right" answer to any question). But seminary provides a safe and sacred space to ask a question that seems logical but does not always fly in the local congregation (e.g., Why did God even put the fruit on the tree if Adam and Eve were not supposed to eat it?). It may border on heresy. Seminary, then, may be the place for people who want to ask difficult questions of the biblical text and of the Christian faith—even if those same people ultimately want to arrive at some level of unified belief or expression.

I liken the seminary experience to the preproduction stage play. My wife and I went to see the Broadway musical version of *The Color Purple* for our wedding anniversary one year. We marveled at the seemingly flawless performance. I remember walking out of the show wondering, *How long did they rehearse to put on such a perfect performance?* I was privy to see the results, but the cast and crew had put in countless hours of work to make the performance possible. The stage construction must have taken months. The composer and lyricist invested countless hours in creating the musical score. The actors worked for weeks on their lines, learned the vocal parts for the songs, and mastered the subtle inflections in voice and mood in stage presence that made the performance believable. Seminary is a bit like those behind-the-scene efforts.

People walk out of the church building after worship service with an impression of their experience. At some point between the pew and the door, the attentive person has judged the merits of the worship experience and sermon. What the faithful church member did not see, though, was the time spent in study. The preacher honed a sense of the elements of worship in seminary so that she could prayerfully and thoughtfully design the order of worship, sensitive to the people in the pew. That member was not there when the preacher's seminary preaching professor offered several critical comments on sermon delivery that made the preacher's better.

Likewise, the church member in the recovery room of the hospital probably does not realize that the minister mastered pastoral counseling through several seminary courses. The member just knows a "good bedside manner." I am not suggesting that ministry is entertainment, but I am comparing the energy and investment that ministers give their work to the effort involved in producing a quality stage performance.

Discern the Call of God's Voice in and over the Crowd

One of the amazing aspects of the passage through seminary is the community of people. Few places similar to seminaries have such creative exchanges about Christianity. Each day in class, faculty and students challenge each other to think deeply about the subject matter. Chapel services call the academic community together to hear from God and reflect. Within these moments, opportunities arise to discern what God is up to in one's life. Listening to God's answers to our questions becomes the key activity for much of the time in seminary. God, what shall I do with this? God, where would you have me to serve? *God, are you calling me to the pastorate? What alternative ministry paths might fit my gifts and passion?* Conversations with colleagues and faculty members, family and church members aid in the discovery process. Spiritual formation and professional development courses also reveal some of the answers. Personality assessments and counseling sessions all help. At the end of the day, the burden/blessing falls on your attentive ear to God's call. Can you hear God in and above the crowd?

Discern the Gifts in You

By now you have wrestled with what God has placed in you to do ministry. I encourage you to match your gifts with your call. The gift of teaching is broad enough to include pastoral ministry and/or ministry as a high school or college instructor. Depending on your belief system, the gift of healing may send you to medical school or into the mental health profession. As a professor, I encourage you to do your homework. And then make the seminary work for you—through electives, internships, and mentors. These opportunities will assist you in discerning what God has placed in you.

Electives. Although you will have some required or core courses, you will earn many of your credits through electives, a diverse range of course offerings. This is where the real fun begins.

You may choose to take a variety of electives in a range of ministry areas. Some seminaries will offer electives within a required subject area (e.g., requiring three electives in biblical studies and two in theology). Other schools will leave the elective options wide open, allowing you to concentrate in a specific area or pursue the greatest breadth of ministry exposure. Think about where God is calling you to serve, and choose wisely. If you are going to be a chaplain, use the electives for pastoral counseling classes. Do you plan to preach? Take several elective courses in preaching. Are you preparing to be a seminary professor? Take courses in the discipline that you may want to teach. Use the electives to equip you for the ministry God has for you.

Internships. Seminary also provides a place in the program for an internship, or what many seminaries call theological field education (TFE). Seminaries accredited by the ATS require students to immerse themselves in a field education experience. The course is essentially a supervised ministry internship. The school or the seminarian selects a ministry setting (church or social service agency, among others), and the seminarian serves at the site for a semester or year. The goal of the program is to give the person hands-on work in ministry. The seminary wants the seminarian to wed theory with practice. If the pastor, congregation, or ministry supervisor is agreeable, all of the parties benefit from the time together. The minister serves the people, learns from the people about "church," and builds relationships that last a lifetime.

Mentors. All of your educational experiences—both in classes and in field education—have the potential to yield a mentor. Among your professors, advisers, and classmates, you may encounter people who can give you guidance and wise counsel. From your TFE supervisor or from an active lay leader in your applied ministry setting, you may glean the experience and insight you need for the next steps in your vocational journey.

I had a number of mentors, but one of my best lessons in pastoral care came from Mr. P. O. Green at the Zion Baptist Church in Richmond, Virginia. I accompanied him to the nursing home. As a young minister and first-year seminarian, I had no script to use. He gently offered suggestions about what to say. He also helped me exit the room gracefully. His vote of confidence opened the door for me to teach and preach in other churches.

Discover Your Resource Circle

Faculty, staff, and students share the learning space at seminary. They create a resource circle for ministry education and service. Along with the in-house offering of resources, the seminary becomes an incubator for professional ministry relationships. The school may connect you with your denomination, which can be a wonderful resource for financial aid, job placement, and mission and ministry opportunities. Some seminaries collaborate with one another and with other organizations and agencies to do ministry in nontraditional ways. For example, Wesley Theological Seminary in Washington, DC, has an internship program that explores faith and politics. That is a great place to have that kind of experience! Each seminary is unique and may have local or national partnerships.

Study to Show Yourself Approved

You will waste a lot of time, money, and energy at seminary if you attend classes but fail to do the work that accompanies those classes. The total educational experience can help you grow as a new minister. Challenging texts stretch and challenge ministers to think. Lectures and class discussions engage the texts and help students to make sense of the information. Accessing library resources, preparing research papers, and developing sample lesson plans equip the minister for service.

In the midst of reading and writing for your studies, remember to pray and reflect your way through seminary. When I was younger, I would hear ministers say about a preacher, "Rev. has the learning *and* the burning." God can and will work with it all.

Contribute to the Community

The seminary faculty and administration need the seminarians to make the school a success. The seminary is at peak performance when all members of the community contribute to it. Without committed students, there are few student-led activities. Participants in the chapels come mainly from the student body in many seminaries. Dialogue in the classroom is necessary for the exchange of serious and diverse ideas. A seminarian's voice can also shape the services that the school offers. Students being present, speaking up, and being collegial make a seminary a better place.

Three Years Will Fly By—Now What?

The question that has guided this book reenters at this point. The average seminary maps a three-year journey for its students. That is the traditional timeline. Three years is not a long time for most of us. All of the anxiety that goes into the first year of seminary will subside quickly. You will find that the ebb and flow of each term and its coursework will zip past. Three years will fly by before you know it. My time did. By the time this publication appears, I will be eleven years removed from my seminary days. I have taught in a seminary for six years at this point. The names and the faces of the students change quickly. The one constant is that people will have to leave the school. It is inevitable. The question, therefore, always looms: Now what?

Thinking about what is next from day one can ease the leap of faith that comes after graduation. The discerning seminarian can make choices throughout the journey. If you see your current career/vocation as ministry, you may remain in that setting after you leave seminary. If you want to transition into another graduate or postgraduate program, you can discern an area of study that grabs your attention during each term. Do not necessarily wait to polish the résumé until after the commencement ceremony ends. Use the school's resources to help you. See the career services counselors. Talk with professors. Meet with denominational representatives. Three years will fly by, so make sure you do not miss the opportunities.

Wonderful educational opportunities are available to you. Your prayer, preparation, and homework on the best path for you will yield a blessing. Such preparation will not only bless you; it will touch the people who await your ministry. Which path should you take? I cannot answer that for you. But know that God has placed ministry gifts in you that will grow with you. You will encounter new people and resources along the way. They will remind you that you are not alone in ministry. You are not without support for the journey.

Questions TO CONSIDER

1. Which method of study do you prefer? What makes it your preference?

2. What is on your checklist for attending a school?

3. How much school is enough for the call on your life?

NOTES

1. See the Council for Higher Education Accreditation video at www.youtube.com/watch?v=a1voHNMQDrk.

2. For a directory of schools, see www.ats.edu.

3. See www.fteleaders.org/pages/fteguide for an in-depth overview of the types of theological schools and degree programs.

CHAPTER 6

Considering Ordained Ministry

Regardless of your vocational path, seminary or personal study, you may seek ordination for your ministry journey. Your pastor may approach you about the subject, or people in the church may question whether you are ordained. You might even be a candidate for a pastoral position at a local church, and the church may require that all candidates be ordained. Or you may see ordination as another step toward fulfilling your call. Whatever the case may be, you want to begin the process of ordination. To be sure, this leads you back to the question that has guided the book: "Now what?"

As a denominational adviser at my seminary, I receive a flurry of inquiries about ordination around March and April of each school year. The closer seminarians get to graduation, the more interested they become in discovering the denomination's ordination requirements. They ask very important questions, but one critical thing most of them fail to ask is, "What is ordination?" This may be the most significant question ministers should ask, for faithful ministers of the gospel have a responsibility to learn the working definition of ordination within their local churches and denominational traditions.

Across local congregations and global Christian traditions, ordination has varied meanings. The Presbyterian Church (PCUSA) differs on ordination from the American Baptists (ABCUSA) on substantive points. The United Methodist Church (UMC) may hold to certain notions that the United Church of Christ (UCC) may dismiss. Is one tradition correct? God knows. What is important is for the new minister to be clear about what the church expects of a minister seeking ordination. Awareness of protocol, processes, and expectations can enhance the minister's experience and appreciation of this celebration within the life of the Christian community. For that is what ordination is: a celebration of God's work in the life of believers.

Ordination in most settings is the affirmation from the community of believers for the minister to live in God's purpose through service to the world. The community invites the minister to be who God called the minister to be. In his book *Ordination: Celebrating the Gift of Ministry,* Stephen V. Sprinkle, Professor of Practical Theology at the Brite Divinity School, argues that ordination is a gift of ministry.[1] Ordination is a unique covenant between God and God's people, the minister included, that commissions a gifted servant to labor in the fields of ministry service.

You might ask, "How is this different from the ministerial license?" In at least a few traditions, the local church approves the licensed minister to exercise his gifts in the local church context. The ministry license comes with a "limited" authority. Some congregations and traditions believe that only ordained leaders should perform certain functions in the life of the church, such as serving Communion, doing baptisms, or officiating weddings and funerals. Many churches consider the ministry licensure period to be a time of preparation. The minister learns and discerns by doing the work of the ministry. But in such settings, the licensure launches an apprenticeship, and it signifies the first official step toward ordination.[2]

Many congregations invite their licensed associate ministers to preach, lead Bible studies, teach Sunday school, and participate in the pulpit during the worship experience. In fact, in some traditions, the license to Christian ministry is specifically a license to preach the gospel. For example, the African Methodist Episcopal Church (AME) has numerous offices through which a minister may preach. Most Christian communions agree, though, that ordination represents a distinct commission in service to the church and world.

Ordination: More Than a Status Symbol

Depending on the tradition that your community embraces, ordination brings together two strands of thought in Christian history—the sacramental and the functional. The sacramental understanding of ordination developed over time in the church. In this view, the minister has received a charge that sets him apart as a representative of the church, but the ordination rite is understood to transfer a grace that imparts upon the minister the gifts and authority for service.

The Protestant Reformation introduced another view of ordination. Reformers spoke of ordination as a function.[3] The functional perspective recognizes that the gifts for ministry are already present in the candidate for ordination, and the ritual is a symbolic affirmation and official acknowledgment of the ordinand's authority for ministry. Why was this new understanding important? The abuse of power by clergy during the early sixteenth century prompted the Reformers to rethink Christian ministry. A sacramental view of ordination had led to identifying clergy as a special class of person, possessed with grace-imparting abilities (e.g., to forgive sin or grant salvation). The functional view rejects the suggestion that ordination effects an intrinsic change in a person. The gifts for ministry are present before the ritual of ordination, and those gifts are functional in nature (e.g., preaching, teaching, compassion). The church merely acknowledges what God has already placed within the person.

In both sacramental and functional approaches to ordination, the minister becomes a person who can handle and administer the sacraments (or ordinances) of the church. The minister's charge makes him a leader that has divine blessing to "stand out" as an agent of Christ. Christians throughout time have considered the ordained ministry the high and holy work of the church. The minister's authority and "power" stem from a divine source that yields divine power. Bishops affirmed early Christian ordinands by the laying on of hands. The practice still exists in both sacramental and functional traditions. Much of the sacramental tradition views the ritual of laying on of hands in a mystical way, wherein the ordinand receives the transference of grace, while in the functional tradition of most Protestant churches, the laying on of hands is seen through a more symbolic lens, as a blessing and setting apart of the new minister for ministry.

I tend to believe that more than a few churches and ministers struggle with the tension between sacramental and functional views of ordination. They believe that there is something special about the minister as well as about the ordained ministry. They also believe that the ministry is not a separate "special" order within the church. The minister is human just like any other person—a conviction expressed through the Methodist principle of "ministers all" and the Baptist celebration of "the priesthood of all believers."

This "tension" about the significance and effect of ordination is alive and well. We see it in some church settings where the licensed minister is not allowed to serve at the Lord's Supper (Eucharist, Communion); only the ordained minister may. The licensed (or provisional) minister, in many traditions, does not perform the marriage ceremony; the ordained minister does.

As mentioned before, context can define practice for a community. The tension between contrasting views of ordination may create what amounts to being a hierarchy of ministry. A person may want ordination because he sees it as an opportunity to change his title. In many settings, the minister goes by "Minister" after licensure and "Reverend" after ordination. The distinction is an attempt by some preachers to help new ministers know their place in the learning process. In such a functional apprenticeship model, the ministry license is something like a driver's permit. In contrast, the ordination is like the driver's license. A permit empowers the apprentice or learner to practice new skills under the close supervision of an experienced teacher. An ordained minister is like a licensed driver, having full autonomy to practice the gifts of ministry without supervision in any number of contexts. Of course, whether licensed for or ordained to Christian ministry, ministers should not lord it over anyone. We are servants to God's people.

Ordained to What?

Ordination, as a gift of ministry, is God's call to service to the Christian minister. Ordination is also the church's call to accountability for the minister's gifts, calling, and vocation in Christian ministry. Now what? The most important question the minister's council in my region asked me was simple yet profound: To what are we ordaining you?

This question should be the foundation of the discernment process for the minister seeking ordination. "Why do you want to be ordained?" may be a more direct question. But "To do what?" is the question that suggests more about your vocational journey. It reflects a belief that ordination is more than the privilege to serve the Eucharist, perform weddings, or bury the dead. The question "Ordained to what?" gets at the specifics of your ministry charge(s). The question calls for a level of vocational clarity that the "why" question can elude.

Pastor: Why do you want to be ordained?

Minister: I want to be equipped to do ministry at a higher level.

Translation: This is the logical next rung on the ministry ladder.

Reflecting on my ordination experience, I realized that I was impatient with my ordination. I believed that it was the logical "next step" in ministry. When I first started thinking of ordination, I was a year away from graduating from seminary. Everyone else was talking about being ordained. That is what you do when you get a seminary degree, right? I even had an answer to the council's question "To what?" but I was not ready to walk into it at that point. I knew that I was called to be a seminary professor. But at that time, I was just beginning my doctoral studies. I did not have a job as a seminary professor. I just had vocational clarity. Did that merit ordination? It all depends on your context. I saw ordination as the next step in the journey. It seemed like a promotion. But the "To what?" question helped me clarify what I believe is the real purpose of ordination. After nearly twenty years of ministry, I get it now—I think.

First, ordination is a *call to accountability*. Ordination, in any tradition, expresses a commitment to give oneself in service to God. There is also mutual accountability between minister and church. The church acknowledges that God has gifted the minister and affirms its investment in him. The ordaining church, local ministers and congregations, and denominational representatives may all participate in this affirmation. An ordained minister, in turn, is accountable to these people. Whether the minister remains in the congregation or goes forth from it, he represents the people who invested in him.

Second, ordination can also be a *celebration of clarity*. Minister and people can see and celebrate the "aha" moment. When people and preacher acknowledge and affirm what God is doing in the life of the church by way of the minister—amen. The celebration can happen, ideally, when the minister and church affirm calling and vocation. It is the collective "We see what you are doing, God, and it is marvelous in our eyes." The minister does not ordain himself. The church ordains, agreeing with God and the minister about the minister's gifts and calling. The ordination itself is a gift. Through the ordination service, the church presents to the called and equipped minister a gift of trust, affirmation, and authority.

Preparing for Ordination

Providing an example of an ordination path here seems necessary. Denominational requirements vary, but some of the tasks are universal. Any person feeling led or invited to be ordained may complete them on the way to ordination. There is, of course, no substitute for prayer and discernment in this journey. No minister wants regret to be a part of his ordination memories. Remember, ordination is a celebration. Preparing for the celebration may create some anxiety, but it should reduce a lot of it as well.

Learn about Your Church's Ordination Tradition

Ordination is primarily a celebration that begins at the local church level. (This may vary with traditions that have bishops.) Depending on your denomination, the candidate may initiate the process with the pastor of the congregation. In some settings, the pastor decides when the time is right for a minister to receive ordination. The process may start with the minister having a conversation with the pastor. (If you are curious about ordination, ask.) Or the pastor may see the gifts in the minister and sense the need to start the process. Context may suggest that either way is correct. It is important, therefore, to know who your church feels should initiate ordination and when. The pastor and church may require that a minister complete seminary before being ordained. A church may use experience as the marker. Some churches may not ordain women. The minister's sexual orientation, age, or marital status could exclude the person from ordination and/or ministry in some places. Interpretations of Scripture and age-old traditions inform rules and practices that the minister needs to know.

While learning these traditions, be sure to check the church's relationship with a denomination. For example, a Baptist congregation may affiliate with one or more national conventions or regional associations. The relationship(s) connects the church and minister to associations of churches and a national family of believers. This relationship could be important for more than one reason. The built-in support group and network a denomination provides is important. The newly ordained minister is not alone. Other laborers in the ministry are seeking to be faithful in the work God has given them. Conferences and convention or association meetings can often provide ministry support. Ministers' groups and functions help create collegial environments and opportunities for ministry partnerships. Some denominations provide support for their ministerial leaders in the form of financial assistance for their initial theological education. They may also support continuing education. In addition, they may have benefits and retirement programs. If you stop your inquiry about ordination at the local church level, you may miss the benefits that come with being a part of a larger church family. Going through a denomination for ordination may also make the process more formal and thorough.

It is also important to note that national church bodies may encourage steps in an ordination process that the local church does not include. Some denominations see their process as an opportunity to establish accountability between the minister and the national body. Requiring seminary, psychological assessments, and ministerial council reviews can be viewed as basic "quality control measures." The local church may or may not share those denominational standards. The minister must decide what path—local or denominational ordination—is best for her.

The local church may have its guidelines for ordination written in its by-laws. A quick trip to the church library or an email request to the church clerk can provide you with a good deal of information. This should not replace conversation with church leadership, however. You will still want to talk to the pastor and, perhaps, other leaders about the process. They may tell you about the "unwritten rules." Have a conversation with one of the ministers the church ordained. What was his experience? This will not define your journey, but it is a point of reference.

Get Your Materials Together

After you learn about the ordination process, gather your materials and do your homework. Dust off your ministerial license and be prepared to present it if needed. Every minister does not receive licensure and ordination within the same congregation. You may need to show your license to the new congregation or submit a letter from your previous pastor. A church may also require you to prepare a paper that details your call narrative and explains your beliefs. If a denomination is involved, you may find this to be the case. The paper will probably include your understanding of God, Jesus, the Holy Spirit, the Bible, and some issues of denominational polity. You may need to submit transcripts and reference letters that display your competency and character for ministry.

The denomination may also require a psychological evaluation and profile for ministry. The purpose of this evaluation is for the minister to understand his ministry strengths and weaknesses with more depth. If the evaluation raises red flags, the discerning candidate and ecclesial body will probably have a conversation to clarify such matters. The evaluating team may come from within the denomination or be an independent contractor. Either way, a minister may benefit from seeing the sessions as an opportunity for vocational clarity.

In some settings, the pastor may tell you to prepare to recite your beliefs and the Scriptures that support them. This will require some studying that may result in pages of notes. You will not go wrong with preparing a faith statement or essay on the Christian faith. The oral presentation does not preclude your preparing a formal document. You may not have to bring it with you, but it can certainly help clarify your thoughts. Remember, you will probably have to share your call story. An organized version of this will help you reduce some of the "dead air" that comes from thinking of what to say next.

Prepare for the Council and Examination

Why do you need this material? You will probably be required to present it to a council of ministers or ministers and laypeople who will examine you. Most ordinations follow this basic procedure. In some cases, you may meet with two councils. There could be a regional ministers' council or commission on the ministry that upholds standards for professional clergy within the denomination. Such a council meets to acknowledge your preparation for ordination at the denominational level. Churches that have a congregational polity will have at least one council. The pastor and church will bring together qualified people from the community to have a conversation with you about your beliefs so that the church family can affirm your calling, gifts, and preparation for ordained ministry. This conversation is one that will challenge you to think deeply about the Christian faith and prompt you to articulate what God is doing in your ministry. The tone and mood should not be antagonistic, but be prepared for everything. There may be people in the room who have concerns or issues that speak volumes about their insecurities, not your ministry.

Follow the Pastor's Lead in Developing the Worship Experience

The ordination service is, for some, the high mark of the celebration. It should be a true worship experience. After you have written the papers, the council reads them, and you "pass" the examination, the community praises God for the gift that is your ministry. Sometimes this all happens in the same weekend. Denominational protocol may caution councils and churches about planning a worship experience before knowing the results of the examination. Make sure you have this information in advance so that your ordination experience will be as worshipful and obstacle-free as possible.

Some churches and denominations have templates for the ordination worship experience. The order of worship may include a liturgy, some formal statements, a sermon, and the conferral of ordination by the laying on of hands. The people who are laying hands on you are usually ordained ministers from the community—including some from your council. You are the "distinguished guest" for the experience. Some churches seat the ordinand in the front pew.

Follow the pastor's lead in the planning of the worship service, and be careful not to offend anyone. If he invites you to select a participant, be prepared to offer names. Some ministers select a favorite seminary professor or ministry mentor. If the pastor wants to know your robe size, share it, because some churches buy newly ordained ministers a ministerial robe. Taking part in the planning with people who are organizing this celebration can help reduce the stress that would keep you from enjoying it.

Follow Up with Denominational Representatives

If you do not include the denomination on the front end of the ordination experience, you may have an opportunity to do so after the worship experience. Some denominations will recognize your local church ordination if you have completed denominational requirements. A letter from your pastor on your behalf and a couple of other steps (e.g., meeting with the regional or executive minister, completing a personnel profile for your denomination's placement service, etc.) could give you standing within your denomination's professional registry. This is, of course, a matter for discernment. Some people do not believe that there is any benefit from denominational relationships. Meet with the pastor and denominational leaders if you have questions about this matter. They can help you think about ordination and the next steps beyond that.

Ordination can be a wonderful blessing for the minister. As stated above, it may be a prerequisite for employment in ministry. Some traditions have no clear process for ordination and placement. But a conversation about ministry placement is a good "now what" after ordination.

Questions TO CONSIDER

1. What is your understanding of ordination? How did you come to that conclusion?

2. With what denominations does your church affiliate? What are their recommendations for ordination candidates?

3. What are the prerequisites for ordination in your local church (if this is the ordaining body)?

NOTES

1. Stephen V. Sprinkle, *Ordination: Celebrating the Gift of Ministry* (St. Louis, MO: Chalice, 2004).

2. One may be surprised to learn that states vary about who can perform weddings. A licensed or ordained minister is able to perform in several states. I am guessing that most states allow religious institutions to decide the matter of license versus ordination.

3. E. Glenn Hinson, "Ordination in Christian History," *Review and Expositor* 78, no. 4 (1981): 485–96.

CHAPTER 7

Where Do I Go from Here?

Ministry Placement

Ministry is not a nice and neat series of steps, as outlined in these chapters. We each create our own steps. In some traditions, the charismatic minister may feel a call and open a storefront church the next day. If denominational standards or church protocol do not intervene, the ambitious pastor may move from the call to the megachurch in a matter of years. Scan your television channels and notice the number of ministers who use the public access channel as a ministry platform. Some of those ministers may have local church support; others have "solo" ministries. The point is this: ministry has no single path. The same God who called Moses, Pharaoh's adopted grandson, called Amos the farmer. Jonah took off in the other direction after hearing his name called for service to Nineveh. When confronted by an angel, Mary offered herself to the Lord after a moment of confusion and curiosity. The suggestions in this book are merely that—suggestions. Nowhere else may this be truer than in this chapter.

Before beginning any conversation on ministry placement, you need to take a moment to reflect. The question that preceded my examination before the minister's council applies here: To what is

God calling you? Hopefully no one enters the ministry flippantly. Entering the ministry job market is also a serious task. Knowing what God called you to do can ease some of the anxieties that come with searching for a position. Are you a pastoral leader? Does that pastorate reside in the parish/congregational setting? Are you more of a pastor-chaplain? Your congregation may be the armed forces, people in correctional facilities, patients and families in a hospital setting, or people in numerous other diverse situations. At the seminary where I teach, I prepare a newsletter for the American Baptist students. I make it a point to challenge them with a vocational reflection moment. Here are some examples:

1. Fill in the blank (honestly): When I leave seminary, I will serve the world as a _____ (pastor, professor, etc.).

2. Stop and take a moment to reflect on what God is calling you to do. Consider these "nontraditional" ministry paths in your moments of prayer and discernment: religious news/opinion blogger, ministry media consultant, church website developer.

3. Do you feel like the seminary library is the best place in the world? Do you quietly dream that the whole world would be ordered by the Dewey Decimal system? Be a theological librarian. Learn more about being a librarian, and consider a two-year program in library science (www.ala.org/ala/educationcareers/careers/paths/index.cfm).

4. Writing the books that people read on a subject is a fun way to express one's vocation. How are your editing skills? If you enjoy reading and revising someone's work, be an editor. Consider the world of religious publishing. Take a look at these examples:

   a. Write or edit Sunday school or vacation Bible school curriculum.

   b. Blog for an online religious publication.

   c. Write or edit for one of the major denominational presses: Abingdon (United Methodist), Westminster John Knox

(Presbyterian USA), Pilgrim Press (UCC), Judson Press (American Baptist), Augsburg Fortress Press (Evangelical Lutheran Church of America), etc.

d. Write for a religious periodical such as *Christian Century* or one of *Christianity Today*'s family of magazines.

5. The world is in need of university chaplains-pastors, so consider campus ministries if:

a. You are concerned about the spiritual and vocational exploration of adults.

b. You are interested in helping others navigate faith questions in academic settings.

c. You are able to communicate with diverse religious groups.

Have you ever considered these paths? Well, there are these and then some. You may even feel called to the classroom. Your seminary professor might have tapped you on the shoulder and said, "Have you thought about earning a PhD?" Ministry comes in many shapes and sizes. Some ministers will lead a local church, yes, but others will teach in a college, seminary, or university. Some will minister as chaplains in the military, in hospitals, with hospice patients, with first responders (e.g., fire and police), in workplaces, or on educational campuses. Others will serve as social workers, medical missionaries, denominational staff, or something else. What is God calling *you* to do?

The Quickest Path between Two Points?

Mathematicians will tell you that the shortest distance between two points is a straight line. Shortest means fastest and best, right? That may be true in most physical contexts, but ministry placement often zigzags. Even for the same type of position, applicants may experience different routes. The formal system of placement is a clear process that seems to privilege none but the qualified. The informal system is diverse. Doors may open by a kind elder passing your name on to a search committee or your pastor recommending you to fill an interim position. The phone tree or "incidental" invitation to preach may cause you to end up as a part of a pastoral search. Or you may choose to take initiative by going to denominational websites and signing up to receive biweekly position listings. With a few taps on the keyboard, you can encounter numerous ministry listings. There is more than one way to begin your search.

Denominational Programs

In some church traditions, including Baptist conventions, the local church is the entity that searches out and calls a pastor. In other denominations, the national body guarantees most clergy placement in a church. Bishops see to it that qualified candidates move to congregations in need of a pastoral leader. That covers those called to the pastorate. But what do the rest of the ministers do?

Some denominations have programs that secure ministers' vocational information to distribute to inquiring institutions or churches. An example of this is the profile system in the American Baptist Churches USA (ABCUSA). A seminarian fills out a personnel profile that becomes an electronic résumé for personnel services to place in a database. When partnering churches and institutions need a minister that fits your gifts and ministry preferences, the database system automatically sends your profile. The American Baptist Personnel Services office encourages ministers to update their profiles every three years for a nominal fee. Other denominations post positions and store candidates' résumés online. Some regional bodies within denominations may host listening sessions to pair candidates with institutions and churches. Such events vary based on location and leadership in the area. Some regions may not have the staff to offer such events. Incidentally, religion scholars can look to academic guilds for positions in seminaries, universities, and colleges. Check their websites.

Networks and Connections

Official channels and denominational protocols aside, all search processes seem to have some wiggle room in them. Do not underestimate the value of relationship building as part of your vocational journey. The same people who have been helpful mentors may also provide an inside track on a key ministry opening. Yes, even in ministry there are insiders who know someone who knows someone else close to a search. Local church leaders may quietly advertise an open position at a sister congregation before the official search commences. Denominational executives often hear about a church in transition or a promising candidate before a search committee has even formed.

These kinds of informal networks function in ways that outsiders to the process cannot see. When you are among those outsiders, the process can be discouraging. Take heart, however, and trust that people are willing to hear God's voice about the direction of the searches. Be proactive about your own networking efforts, but be authentic and ethical in how you make connections. Getting a promoter or emissary on your behalf might be your way to the top of a search committee's stack of applicants, but be prayerful lest you tamper with the integrity of the process. Knowing where that line is drawn is important.

Putting Your Best Foot Forward

As in any job search, the pursuit of a ministry placement requires the preparation of basic tools—key documents that will introduce you as the candidate to the search committee or interview panel. Long before you speak with a human being, you will typically make your first impression through your cover letter and résumé or curriculum vitae.

Your Cover Letter

Even in a technological age where many applications are submitted via website or email, the traditional cover letter is still a powerful means of introducing yourself to a prospective employer. It speaks on your behalf in spaces where you cannot physically represent yourself and is the most personalized overture of your literary introduction.

Each cover letter you send should be tailored to the ministry position for which you are applying. Read the job listing carefully before writing your letter. The listing probably includes helpful information about the church or organization. Note any brief descriptions of the membership, staff size, denominational affiliation, ministry duties and daily tasks, and salary. Such information will help you determine whether you wish to pursue the position. If you do apply, you can construct a cover letter that speaks to the details of the listing.

Notice the language of this listing:

> The Medical Center seeks a skilled professional to lead the chaplaincy unit. The successful candidate will have a master's degree in a counseling field and a certificate in clinical pastoral education. Applicants should also have three to five years of experience in the profession.

In this case, your graduate-level education and related experience in various counseling positions need a prominent place in the cover letter. So, after establishing your name and the position for which you are applying, your letter might read:

> My master of divinity studies and clinical pastoral education provided a foundation for my first chaplaincy position. I eventually served for six years as assistant chaplain at Greater Health Hospital. I worked closely with the medical staff to encourage and counsel patients and to listen to and console their families.

Each position asks for something different. Use the description to identify desired skills and to match your qualifications for that opportunity. The cover letter allows you to explain more conversationally what your résumé or curriculum vitae presents in a list of names, titles, and dates.

Consider this description for a pastoral search:

> The Proctor Memorial Baptist Church was founded in Richmond, Virginia, in 1955. The church has had an important place in the life of this community for more than a half century. Proctor Memorial considers itself a theologically moderate church that focuses on com-

munity development and social engagement. The membership also believes that it is vital to call people to a personal faith commitment to Christ. The members aim to provide a ministry to strengthen families of all socioeconomic levels and to equip them to grow together in Christ and go into the world for Christ. Declining membership has increased the church's necessity for visionary leadership.

This church is looking for a pastor. What details stand out in their listing? A church would not take the time to mention these things if they were not important. Does "theologically moderate" strike you as too narrow, too liberal, or just right? Are you motivated or discouraged by "declining membership"? Would you describe yourself as a "visionary" leader? If so, what examples can you provide to illustrate that leadership? What experience, if any, do you have with ministries related to community development, discipleship, and outreach or missions?

It may also be worth noting what is not included in a ministry listing. What details are omitted (number of members)? What requirements are not specified (education or experience)? What else is missing—and why? Perhaps this congregation is not concerned with a seminary education or a minimum number of years of experience—or maybe they assume that the necessity of an MDiv is so obvious that it is not worth mentioning. You cannot know the answers for sure, but it would be worth your while to note what is missing and follow up at your interview.

Your Résumé

Most adults are familiar with the essential résumé—usually a one- or two-page document that is a professional summary of a person's education and work experience. If you have never compiled a résumé before, you will find numerous books and websites that can help you put your information together. Different templates will emphasize different elements—education if you have limited experience, or experience if you lack formal education. Some will emphasize skills; others will focus on your objectives. Your résumé strategy will be determined in large part by who you are as a person and what you are seeking in a ministry position.

The basic information is the same on all résumés: your full name and ministry title (Minister, Reverend, Elder, Deacon); your contact information, including mailing address, email address, and telephone number(s); your education, including degrees earned and concentrations studied; and your relevant or recent employment history. You may also want to include a list of skills or qualities that may be pertinent for the position. For example, highlight your administrative abilities for an executive pastor position and emphasize your people skills for a chaplaincy. If space allows—a résumé is traditionally just one or two pages long— provide the names of a few references. An alternative to that is to state at the bottom of the last page, "References available upon request." Then be prepared with a separate document that lists reference names and contact information.

Two tips as you think about formatting this document. First, use the résumé to speak to what the job description indicates the institution or church is looking for. If the church wants a pastor concerned about Christian education, highlight your years of instruction for the adult Sunday school class or midweek Bible study. A chaplain candidate might consider placing the clinical internship right below her education history, relegating a lengthier but less relevant professional history in finance to a brief bullet point at the end. You do not want to make the committee search too hard for the information it wants to find. The résumé does not even need to include every place of employment or educational experience. Focus on a summary comprised of the most relevant and impressive highlights of who you are.

Curriculum Vitae

Especially if you are pursuing a ministry position in theological education, a Latin word has to find its way into the text at this point: *curriculum vitae*. More familiarly called a CV, this document is a far more in-depth overview of your professional life. If the résumé is a kind of highlights reel, with just a page or two that lists degrees earned and positions held, the CV is more like a documentary miniseries. Some CVs consist of ten or twenty pages with an exhaustive listing of educational and professional achievements. A CV will include the résumé highlights—education and work experience—but also any awards or honors, your teaching and publication credits, and your memberships or affiliations with other bodies (honor societies, professional associations, etc.).

In the CV, specify not only the schools you attended and the degrees earned, but any honors bestowed, scholarships won, or awards given. Provide not only the places where you have worked and the titles you held, but also the committees you chaired, the teams you participated in, and the initiatives you spearheaded. List any workshops you facilitated, seminars you attended, or presentations you made. Note any articles or essays you wrote and where they were published. Highlight any books to which you contributed or publications for which you served as editor. Include any classes you taught, especially if you created the syllabus and designed the course.

The CV is a living document that grows as you do. The longer you live and work and minister, the more impressive (in most cases), the CV becomes. If you are a new seminary graduate or if this is your first ministry position, you would be wise to use the résumé format for now. But start building your curriculum vitae; it may not be long before you are amazed by the experiences and achievements it features.

The cover letter and résumé or CV can get you in the door for an interview, so be intentional and direct in their presentation. I cannot say this enough: speak to what the description requests. And do not be afraid to get help in this process. If you are a student or alum of a seminary or university, go to its career resource center and ask a professional to review your application materials. A friend or objective family member may also catch some mistakes or offer good advice. The little things can help your application stand out in a ministry employment search.

Research the Institution/Church

While you may begin the research on a church or institution before submitting an application, pre-interview research should include extensive study. In this age of instant information, it is easy to learn a little about anything. Online resources can help the searching minister learn more about employment opportunities and sites. An Internet search can give a landscape view of the neighborhood of the employment site and provide demographics of the area as well as information on the cost of living there. The church or institution may have a website that lists even more details. And online newspapers may yield still more information about the potential place of ministry employment. Use all this information to determine how you "fit" in this place. Is the cost of living too high for you? Can you find a good school system for your children? A thorough search can help you think through these concerns. What is the congregation size? What is the size of the staff at this place? Will you have to do it all? Salary may not be as important to you as having time for family and self-care. If you do not have a placement checklist, now would be a good time to make one. Before you use up anyone's time with an interview, see if you are a good fit for the place.

There are at least two ways to approach an employment search. First, you may be looking for the "right" position, one that will allow you to exercise your gifts. Second, you may be seeking any position, anything that will pay the bills until the right position comes along. The first may be ideal, but we may find ourselves in the second position. In the current economy, you may just want a job. You may need to consider programs for interim ministry if urgency outweighs patience and fit for a ministry position. Generally there is an understanding in this arrangement that the interim minister has a temporary charge. The interim can then seek long-term ministry employment that begins after the arrangement without adversely affecting congregational health. Timing could be everything in this regard. In either circumstance, research can be an important step toward getting an interview and landing a position. If you are applying to a church, you may also want to call the region office or association president or moderator for information. These staff people and/or officers can sometimes present an objective observation about the congregation.

Preparing for the Interview

If you are one of the few people that an institution, agency, or church selects for an interview, congratulations. This can be an accomplishment in and of itself. National searches can produce hundreds of applications from candidates seeking positions, but an interview means that you are receiving serious consideration for the position. After judging the opportunity to be a good fit, get ready to put your best you forward in the interview.

Some employing agencies or institutions split the interview process into two parts, the phone interview and the "campus" interview.

The Phone Interview

The phone interview is a unique phenomenon. You face the challenge of hearing and responding to questions without the aid of body language, so you have to interpret responses over a telephone line. Some candidates complain about this. They would rather see the faces of the search committee, because their faces can often reveal more or less what the candidate needs to say. Interviewees want to know if the interviewers smile or cringe after a response. This can be a tough way to interview, but just relax and be you. That will be the best way to approach the interview. Pace yourself and be prepared for awkward pauses and deafening silence. Do not read too much into these moments. It may just be that the committee is deviating from its script or someone has forgotten to chime in at the appropriate time. (By the way, the good news is that technology now provides an opportunity to have a long distance face to face. Web programs such as Skype give search committees and applicants a chance to see each other's smiling faces.)

I also have two quick suggestions that apply to both the phone and campus interviews. First, make sure you write down and ask the questions you want answered. There is a point in almost every interview where the candidate can ask the interviewer questions. Take advantage of this opportunity. Find out from the source what you want to know. Do not, however, ask a question that you could have answered with simple research. It will be embarrassing if you find that you could have looked at the sign on the front door to see how many worship experiences the congregation has on Sunday mornings.

Second, be prepared to respond to surprising questions. I once interviewed for a pastoral position. I sat before the interview team, and someone asked me: "When you go out to dinner, do you order lemonade or ask for a bowl of lemons and a glass of water?" Everyone in the room looked at the person with a curious stare. I asked the person for clarity. He was very serious. The response was simply this: "I want to know if you are a thief. I want to see if you rob the restaurant by trying to make your own lemonade." Who can prepare for such unique and off-hand questions? But do your best to frame a tactful response. Also, be aware that questions about your age and marital status are generally off-limits. The nature of such taboo questions could depend on where you apply—for example, public or private sector.

I call some questions elimination questions. "How much would you expect us to offer you for a salary?" If you participate in a pastoral search, you should probably defer any questions about salary until the church is ready to present you with an offer. If a committee asks early in the process, the committee may intend for it to keep you in or knock you out of the running. A person may ask a question to get you to side with her position. "Women should not be in the pulpit! Don't you agree, Reverend?" You may be wading into a war before you start your first day. Know which hypothetical questions require a direct response. "How would you bring in more young people?" So many things to consider, but you can manage these tasks.[1]

The In-Person Interview

The on-site interview provides an opportunity for you to be in the room and make your best case. Your charisma and influence should complement the wonderful résumé and cover letter you submitted. Be sure to pay attention to the details that come with this type of interview.

Getting to the Interview. Be aware of your travel details and expenses. Know when and where you are interviewing and how you will arrive at the place. Will the church reimburse you for your travel expenses? Do you need a projector and computer for a PowerPoint presentation? Whom do you talk to about these matters? Find out this information to make for a smooth transition. Does the tenor of the interview allow for business casual dress or is it all "get down to business"? Knowing this information before your interview will ease some of your anxiety.

Preparing for the Interview. Find out the details of the actual interview. For example, some churches may ask you to present a Bible study or preach during the weekend of the interview. If you take the path of the religious scholar, a college may ask you to present a lecture to a class or group of professors. You might have to plan an ecumenical worship experience as a hospital chaplain candidate. The nonprofit may ask you to present a development/fundraising strategy. To be sure, you will need to be prepared. Knowing how to prepare is an important step to make the interview a success.

Sift through books at your public library for more detailed advice on interviewing. And check with your mentors about the best and most efficient ways to navigate the interview process. Once you get the ministry position, you will have another set of questions and issues to address.

Questions TO CONSIDER

1. What are the ministry placement practices in your denomination or local church community?

2. What are some of your initial hopes for ministry placement?

NOTE

1. See Appendix A for sample interview questions.

PART THREE

Reflecting on Ministry Matters

CHAPTER 8

Salaries, Service, and Sabbath

I can just imagine Isaiah after experiencing the Lord's awesome display of glory in the smoke-filled temple. He remembered that he had told the Lord, "Here am I; send me!" Now he had to begin the work. Likewise, when a place of ministry calls you the time will arrive for you to get to work. But first a few things need to happen—negotiating your salary, transitioning to your place of service, and finding the right balance for your lifestyle. "The Laborer Deserves to Be Paid," a yearly publication from the Ministers and Missionaries Benefits Board (MMBB) of ABCUSA, argues the point for me. A minister's service is worthy of pay.

Accepting the call can be a difficult moment. Discerning *where* to go and *when* to go can be an anxiety-filled event. I recommend Marcia Patton and Riley Walker's *When the Spirit Moves: A Guide for Ministers in Transition* (Judson Press, 2011). This is a wonderful resource for thinking through some of these matters. If this is your first charge, relocating, meeting new people, and feeling worthy of the work can be daunting. Even if this is your second or third position, you may have the same anxieties. The fears that come with any transition can be a bit much at times. (Talk with a mental health professional if necessary.) We are prone to ask, "Am I good enough?" or "Will they listen to me?" Fears may crop up due to insecurities, but if a church called you after a thorough examination of your transcripts and résumé or curriculum vitae, phone calls to your references, and a diligent interview, you are probably qualified.

Unless you are a permanent volunteer, you will need to establish your salary. Here is the big moment! The key people have offered you the position, and they ask you into a smaller conference room or office to have a conversation about your compensation package. What do you do? You should have already done your homework on this subject. It is inexcusable to go into the conversation without having a figure in mind. This is nothing new for the second-career minister, and you probably have nothing to fear with the compensation dialogue. If you plan to work in the church, however, compensation will probably have a slightly different feel to it. Let us think briefly about the preparation needed to reduce the stress of the moment. Begin with the end in mind.

Homework for the Salary Negotiation

Several resources exist to help you prepare your figures for compensation. Once when I was interviewing for a position, a church brought me in to talk about "the numbers." Before I went to the church, my region executive, Dr. Arlo Reichter, told me to contact the Ministers and Missionaries Benefits Board, an organization founded by American Baptists in 1911 to support retired and disabled ministers. Its ministry has supported the work of ministry through retirement programs and medical and dental benefits.[1] Other denominations have similar agencies or organizations—sometimes called "pension boards"—that can help with this type of planning.

The MMBB representative for our region was Dr. Sara Day. She met with me at the annual gathering that year. I told her about my applicant status in the pastoral search and gave her a little information about the church before we met. During our meeting, she convinced me to enroll in the retirement program. She also gave me the financial demographics of similar-sized congregations in the area. The meeting helped me tremendously by giving me a better understanding of what I should request in compensation and why I should ask for it. I felt as if I had studied for my exam.

If this is your first ministry job in a church, you have a few more resources and things to consider. The Consumer Price Index is a wonderful resource that gives you information about the rate of inflation in localities. You can use it to see the value of your dollar where you will do ministry. It may also help you see the compensation of professionals who have similar responsibilities. You may compare your skill set and role to those of a professional with comparable education and leadership tasks. If you are considering a ministry in the academy, the Association of Theological Schools and the *Chronicle of Higher Education* publish the average salaries of staff and instructors at institutions (see www.ats.edu and chronicle.com).

Experience can be an important issue in compensation decisions. The assistant professor in higher education starts at a lower salary than professors at a higher rank. The same system holds true for most first ministry positions. Of course, experience is not the only factor. A search committee should also consider your education, because your education has some monetary value in most cases. Consider these factors before determining a final number.

Another concern for new ministers is understanding the makeup of the compensation package. For ministers who seek a position with an organization outside the parish setting (e.g., chaplaincy with hospital or military, nonprofit agencies, seminary, college, and/or theological librarians), compensation may be straightforward—an annual salary or wage with a traditional benefits package of health and retirement plans. The compensation package for the church leader is constructed quite differently. Here is an example of such a package for a pastoral leader:

Salary	$25,000
Housing*	$20,000 or parsonage allowance
Social Security Offset	$5,000
Total	$50,000

*The housing allowance may be nontaxable. Check with a tax professional.

Some churches pay money directly to a company or organization for the minister's retirement and health benefits. Churches may include continuing education, books, and travel allowances in some minister's packages. Getting the assistance of a tax professional can help you think through the details of your compensation package.[2] Negotiating what is right for you is important.

All of this information is significant if you are thinking about a salary package for the first time. Make sure you understand your philosophical approach to salary negotiations. You could have one of at least three approaches. First, you may be happy just to have a paid position. "They will actually pay me to do what I love? Wow!" Or "I have a job! I have a job! I have a job!" In this approach, you accept whatever the church or institution offers without question or consideration of practical matters. I do not recommend this approach. You should at least learn how other people understand the value of the position.

Second, you may ask for what you want, knowing that your ideal salary may be notably higher than what the church can afford. This strategy presumes, however, that by asking for what you want, you will at least get what you need.

Third, you may ask for what you need and make your case for it. In this approach, you will want to be careful not to undervalue yourself and your ministry. Similarly, you will want to be well informed about your new community and lifestyle so that you do not underestimate your needs. The ethics of negotiation are up to you and your understanding of what God is calling you to do. Again, I recommend a book such as *When the Spirit*

Moves. The book gives more detail and clarity about such matters as compensation packages.

Sabbath for the Minister

Every minister needs an opportunity for renewal. Even the Lord rested on the seventh day, and Jesus told his disciples to come apart from the crowds and rest awhile. So surely a minister's vacation is justified. But what about a sabbatical, an extended leave for renewal, research, and reflection? Depending on what the institution or congregation asks of the minister, such opportunities are often brief. From multistaff church pastors to seminary scholars, ministers find there is a premium on this type of renewal and reflection time. Ministry is a thought- and strategy-intensive vocation. Ministers give time to sermon and/or Bible study preparation, strategic planning for the churches or agencies they serve, management of staff and leading laypeople, and the care of souls, which requires an empathy and compassion that can make a person weary. So ministers can benefit from an extended leave—something more than a few weeks of vacation.

The new minister should consider the sanctity of the time she spends away from her ministry charge. Though it is too early to enjoy the benefit of an extended leave or sabbatical, guarding one's time away from the place of ministry is very important.

A period of renewal and reflection can breathe new life into the minister's work. Make this a part of your ministry package. Negotiate for six to nine months of sabbatical time that will begin after you have served five to seven years of service. As a seminary professor, I have realized the need for space to do such reflecting. If I want to offer new information to students, something that reflects a larger perspective than my own, I need time to gather sources and do research. The pastoral counselor who wants to learn new counseling methods will not master them overnight. The creative and relevant ministry publisher has to study in detail the market dynamics of electronic publishing versus the printed text. Where does a person find the time to do all of this, fulfill other daily responsibilities, and remain healthy? A sabbatical is a way to address such details.

Introducing a sabbatical into your ministry life plan can benefit you and the people you serve or will serve. After a period of five to seven years of service, a sabbatical of—at least—three to six months (try for 6–9) could generate new life.[3] Do your best to include a Sabbath in your compensation package and ministry habits. Plan and file the following suggestions in your future resources drawer.

Plan

Remember to communicate your needs to your ministry partners. The conversation about a Sabbath period can happen at the start of your ministry. Find out if a sabbatical is a familiar practice at your place of service, and if it is not, but you see the need for it, make your case.

Another part of the planning comes in the form of interim ministry. What responsibilities will the people you serve take on during your sabbatical? Will the agency or institution find someone to take your caseload or fill the pulpit? Is that your responsibility? The earlier the conversation takes place, the easier it may be to transition without concerns. Addressing the questions on the front end can reduce some of the stress and separation anxiety.

Funding

With your sabbatical planned years in advance, you will have time to search for funding your Sabbath leave. The Louisville Institute (www.louisville-institute.org) has been a leader among charitable organizations in investing in pastoral study leaves. Scholars of religion can find funding from donors who seek to understand Christian practices and American religious life. Other organizations have interests that may intersect the work you do. Keep this in mind when you are making your plans. See if your denomination provides assistance. This database of information will come in handy at some point.[4]

Evaluating the Journey

Remember to journal about the experience. After taking a Sabbath leave, you and other interested parties will want to know one thing: What did you get out of the experience? Putting your experience in writing and presenting the fruits of your journey will invite others to see your growth. Keeping a journal during your sabbatical will allow you to document your experiences and accomplishments. Summarizing and interpreting your journal entries will save you from a last-minute report that does not reflect the value of the leave.[5]

Serving in the Ministry

Ministry in any capacity is a challenge. Developing sermons, caring for people, or being such a public figure takes time and energy. Your first full-time ministry tasks will fill your time. At first sight, ministry can seem like a profession for the solo superhero. It may be easy to approach ministry as you did seminary—by hitting the books and studying hard for sermons, counseling preparation, administration and leadership, conflict resolution, and strategic planning. But you are not alone in your ministry. No matter what your context, the minister is part of a team—even in a solo pastorate or a solitary chaplaincy position. Where you lack a staff or similar organizational support, create your own team. You will need them! Here are a few people to look to for support in ministry:

Family and friends. In many cases, family members are the people who have stuck with you since the beginning. A spouse, children, parents, close relatives, and friends who are closer than a brother or sister can help you stay grounded. Being available to keep the lines of communication open is my number one suggestion. Loved ones will remind you that there is more to life than the work at the church or other place of ministry. When you come home to hugs or messages from a partner, children, parents, siblings, or other loved ones, you remember that you have people in your corner.

Mentors. Remember the people who walked with you in the early days of your call. Patient and discerning mentors are your partners in the ongoing journey. Learn from their knowledge and experience. They can help you see what your bias and intimacy with a situation obstruct.

Colleagues. Regardless of your ministry profession, you will work with other people. How closely you choose to work with them is the question. Colleagues, particularly in ministry, can be a support system. Religious scholars will benefit from a writing support group. The local ministers' council is a built-in community that can help pastors learn the lay of the land. Professional guilds for chaplains and pastoral counselors offer a network of people with similar vocational interests. Meeting and working with these people are opportunities for collegial support and accountability. Knowing that you have resource people in your corner is essential.

Denomination Staff. Some of your greatest allies in ministry are denominational representatives who can point you toward resources for ministry. Most likely, some of your local church's offerings support the denominational judicatory in your area. They are paid to support you, so take advantage of their knowledge and resources. This is one of the blessings of being connected to a denominational family. In many places, regional staff members are former local church pastors who have experience working in congregational settings. When I served the regional staff of American Baptists in Wisconsin, I visited with pastors, designed orientation events for them and their associate ministers, and kept them informed about seminary support and ministerial benefits. That is the job of these staff persons. Let them support you.

God's People. Ministers serve the people of God in whatever ministry context they find themselves. And God's people are often a source of blessing for the minister. In moments when we do not expect it, we receive encouragement and inspiration from the people we serve. The thank-you cards, the casserole dishes, and the brief phone calls or emails remind us that someone values our work. In the parish setting, some congregations will demonstrate their love and appreciation by annual (or periodic) recognition of the pastor's anniversary. You may also experience the blessing of witnessing people's lives as they celebrate and grieve and as they grow incrementally in faith and love and life. Receive those blessings with joy.

Mapping the road to a successful ministry starts with understanding the details. Remember, there are resources and resource people who can help you think through these matters. From salary negotiation to Sabbath leaves, you are not alone in ministry. Position yourself right now to enter ministry equipped for your journey.

Questions TO CONSIDER

1. Identify a resource person who has knowledge of pastoral compensation. What questions would you have for this person?

2. How well do you guard your time for reflection, family, and enjoyment?

3. What are some best practices that you want to integrate into your ministry service?

NOTES

1. I became aware of the MMBB during the Orientation to American Baptist Life Conference in Green Lake, Wisconsin, in October of 2000. American Baptist leaders established the conference to help seminarians and new pastors learn about the denomination.

2. See www.mmbb.org for worksheets and guides to help you think through these matters.

3. The Ministers Council of the American Baptist Churches USA suggests that a minister take two to three months for every five to seven years of service. See "Planning a Sabbatical Study Leave," www.ministerscouncil.com/Sabbaticals/sabbatical_planning.aspx (accessed August 3, 2012).

4. See Robert M. Franklin, *Another Day's Journey: Black Churches Confronting the American Crisis* (Minneapolis: Fortress, 1997). Chapter 5 begins a conversation about resources for ministry. Franklin worked for a charitable organization and gives tips for developing a proposal.

5. Integrity will probably remind you of the need to stay in your ministry location for at least a year after you return from the leave.

CHAPTER 9

Thoughts on Success in Ministry

Throughout the centuries, Christian ministers have changed the world. They have touched countless people on a personal level and have founded entire social and ecclesial movements as well. Christian ministers have done much good in the world. Because of this, success has different connotations in different contexts. What one person defines as success in ministry may fall short of another person's definition. But I feel it necessary to challenge the reader to consider a working concept that debates or converses with the ideas in this chapter.

What is success in ministry? How does it look or sound? How does it enhance and empower the lives of the people we encounter? Success, I believe, comes forth when we put forward our best selves. Striving for success, then, means that we should be aware of some ministry pitfalls and the opportunities to create best practices.

Pitfalls and Stumbling Blocks

Life will have its moments of imbalance. Demands on our time and spirit may sometimes push us to a constant state of overcompensation. In other words, we can never do enough to catch up or make up for lost time. But that does not stop us from trying. We wear ourselves out and feel guilty for taking time to recover or enjoy life. Some of us travel with our work cell phones connected at all times (even on vacations) and allow "ministry" to invade our lives in an instant. Schedules filled with commitments leave us too tired to rest. But it is only the twisted sense of self that suggests that we remain "on call" 24/7. Unrealistic expectations from others or ourselves can lead us into a rat race that has no real purpose.

But dedication and balance can leave us standing assured that we can give our best. The commitment and motivation to serve coupled with the freedom that comes from a life of balance yields the potential for a successful ministry. I can give my all because I am the emotionally and spiritually rested, healthy person God needs me to be. Is this easier said than done? Yes! But it is an ideal that we should not compromise.

Seeking Dedication and Balance in Ministry

A good place to start the conversation is the implicit and expressed contract you sign when you say yes to God and the ministry as vocation. The surrendering of one's life to God's will is an important step in the journey, for you are agreeing to accept where God leads you and the work God desires you to do. You are also accepting the people God calls you to serve. You are saying yes to a life of sacrifice through service. Since this is the case, you must ask yourself, "Am I up to this?"

Among the array of call narratives I have heard, Dr. Rolen L. Womack's may be one of the most impressive. Womack, the founding pastor of Progressive Baptist Church in Milwaukee, Wisconsin, had a good career in corporate America. He and his wife, an educator, were successful professionals in Houston, Texas. After hearing God's call, he sought more clarity. The clarity he received led him to Milwaukee without the promise of a job. He gave up a nice, expensive home in Texas and left a job that helped finance a comfortable living. After moving to Milwaukee, he took on some odd jobs to make ends meet. He also enrolled in seminary to prepare himself for pastoral ministry. More than twenty-five years later, the Progressive Baptist Church is a healthy congregation that serves the Milwaukee community. Did Womack sign up for this? Yes. Though not one of us knows what a ministry journey will bring, saying yes means committing to whatever the journey will reveal.

From the moment you share your call with the pastor or church elder, you are embracing the fact that ministry is more than a notion. Dedicated ministers of God say, "Here am I; send me!" (Isaiah 6:8) even though we are not aware of everything we are signing on for at that moment. We become the helpers who give ourselves to the study of God's presence in human existence. We teach, preach, and embody the product of our interpretations and results of our learning. We make real how we understand God's movement in the lives of people. Whether we are chaplains, Christian educators, or missionaries, we dedicate our time and resources to this task. As ministers, we say yes to making God's presence known in the moral order. We are agents of change who look for the good in people and encourage them to live into the better. All of this is a part of our commitment of saying yes to God. That yes means that we are willing to serve God's people. So dedication and discernment go hand in hand.

The dedicated minister will seek to understand what the ministry holds. The word *discernment* appears several times in this book. I cannot stress enough how important this activity is for the minister. We are continually called to understand how that looks. This requires discerning minds, hearts, and ears. Can we hear God through the crowd? Since we are not programmed robots, we stumble in our search for clarity. We may try out certain ministry positions that do not fit our gifts and passions. We may misread what our context tells us. But we have an opportunity to learn from these mistakes.

Creating Your Best Practices

With every breath we take, we have the potential to hear anew what God desires of us. Seek out accountability partners who will tell you the truth about you. Have the critical conversations you need to invent and/or reinvent your definition of ministry. Think about the activities and tasks that motivate you. Why do they give you energy? What are they telling you about you and your ministry preferences? What are the ministry activities that bore you or wear you out? Seek ministry positions in which those tasks are not so prominent. It is hard to be effective and successful in ministry if you are serving in areas you would rather avoid. Know that about yourself, and strive to be in a ministry position that highlights your gifts.

As a fan of the Star Wars movies, I always note the times that the characters reference "the Force." The Force has a light and dark side. The light represents the better aspects of human existence. The dark side displays the worst in humanity. The Force, the power that surrounds and informs all of life, requires balance. Without being too philosophical, people with the power of the Force are to have the discipline and strength of character many people celebrate as the ideal. Balance is a good thing. But who defines balance?

Please do not leave the definition of balance in life to anyone else. You alone can and should define what balance means for your life in ministry. You know you better than anyone in this world. No one else can tell you what makes you happiest and what wounds your spirit the most. You know what gives you the healthy energy you need. To be sure, you also know what kind of workload you can handle well. If we are honest with ourselves, the vision that we project of ourselves does not always match reality. Our cape and tights do not make us bulletproof machines with unending energy. We may, therefore, need the assistance of support people and mental health professionals to help us create definitions for ourselves.

Notice my wording for this point. Others can help us create our definition of balance but not define it for us. A minister may have unrealistic expectations for himself founded in what he thinks others expect of him. His life can become unbalanced rather quickly if he thinks he can be everything for everybody in need of help. Thus, defining balance for oneself can make a world of difference.

The form this balance takes may look different for different people, but the results will have a similar effect on each minister's well-being. The minister who arrives at a state-of-life balance has learned that it is okay to say no. The congregation or institution that does not value the minister's time does not value the minister. And boundaries of personal space and time are necessary and justifiable. Cell phones, social networking, and emails can make us accessible at almost all times of the day. But we have the right, and, dare I say, the obligation to make sure that those outlets do not keep us from hearing God's voice. God may be telling us to rest, but we are on the other line or "tweeting." I am not knocking social media. I am just concerned about the ways in which we allow certain activities to offset our need for balance. Binging on certain favorite activities may suggest imbalance in our lives.

To bring your life back into balance, consider creating a schedule for your activities. Build into the schedule time for the things you like to do. Create a window of time to "vegetate," and do not feel guilty about it. The same is necessary for the work you do. Harry Emerson Fosdick, the celebrated former pastor of Riverside Church in New York City, rented a room in an office building near the church and blocked off four hours a day during the week to prepare his sermon. He would use that room to develop the sermons that made him one of the most noted preachers in American Christianity.

People often say that there are not enough hours in the day. Someone may respond, however, "It depends on what you are trying to accomplish." If you need to save the world in one day, nope, there are not enough hours in the day. If you are trying to be a part of God's ever-evolving movement in human history, you have more than enough time. I invite you (and me!) to use it wisely. You do not have to feel guilty about going to the gym or playing golf if you balance out the rest of your day and week. Being preoccupied during your vacation about what you left on your desk is not true relaxation. Why am I saying this? The minister's mind is a funny thing. Sometimes we need permission to know that rest is a legitimate activity. Many of us are victims of various self-inflicted, stress-related illnesses. Kirk Byron Jones's book *Rest in the Storm: Self-Care Strategies for Clergy and Other Caregivers* (Judson Press, 2001) is a good resource for being intentional about this self-care. Define balance for yourself.

Success in Ministry

As we continue to develop a working definition of success, it is important that we address some other topics. In some ways, churches operate like businesses. In corporate structures, getting a promotion means more pay for more responsibility. But what is a minister's promotion? What does advancement look like for a minister?

There are probably several ways to respond to this question. Some of us measure ministry success by examining three key numbers: church attendance, church budget, and pastoral salary. Many ministers will not admit to this. In scanning several pastoral bios, however, you will often notice mention of large memberships or large budgets. There is value in numbers. They are helpful and provide some indication of the ministry's growth. But numbers are only one way to measure success. There are other ways. Let's have a conversation about this matter.

One way to look at ministerial advancement is by measuring the numbers. Some people suggest that this is a very biblical way to approach the task. In Acts 2:41 the writer notes that three thousand people were added to the church after Peter preached. The implication is that the measure of success of the day was the mass of people who joined the church. In some Protestant settings, evangelistic revivalism used and still uses the same "objective" marker to make a case for successful ministry. You know that you are doing God's work when people come to the front of the church to dedicate their lives to Christ. So it goes that the "successful" ministry is the one that fills the seats. A full pew should also equal larger offerings. Larger offerings can erect larger buildings. Success, then, must be a transition from a smaller congregation to a larger one. Or, it is the transition from the lower-paying ministry position to the higher-paying one. Right? To be sure, as a congregation grows, the pastoral leader usually has more responsibility. Among some ministers, there seems to be an apparent trend towards desiring a mega-ministry. The desire may devalue the work and ministry in a smaller congregational setting.

Consider as well the end of Acts 2. The community of believers experienced many signs and wonders among them. They lived in close communion, and persons sold property to sustain the rest of the community. Something happened to them on the inside. One cannot quantify this in numbers. The gospel changed lives and instilled in their fellowship a meaning that was bigger than any one person.

As a seminary professor, I recognize a desire for a mega-ministry among some of the students. For some the vision includes celebrity status and economic security. They hope their paychecks will grow with each ministry charge. Promotion = larger. The numbers are the main sign of ministry effectiveness. To be sure, these students have a concern for people and for their growth and development. Some reason that if the ministry is successful numerically and monetarily it can do more for people. But in practice, they lean more toward filling the pews and growing the budget. In what way might this play out in congregational life?

The church environment sometimes seems to model an election campaign. Each Sunday, the minister has to produce a "stump speech" that rallies the party base. The overarching goals are fund-raising and turnout. If he can keep the people coming and giving, the pastor is destined to be successful on "Election Day." In this case, that is the following Sunday. Sunday becomes a perpetual campaign. The pastor is the incumbent, seeking to reassure the electorate that the financial support and turnout on Election Day (again, the next Sunday) is the right decision. Without the funds, the person cannot fulfill the campaign promises. Without the turnout and support, there will be no campaign funds. The pastor becomes the fund-raiser in chief. The worship experience has to be a campaign rally that people will enjoy. It must promote the party message and tow the party line while catering to the "undecided voters." Does the analogy fit? Unfortunately, it may fit in many places.

We can do both at the same time, the church growth advocate says. I do not argue that we can make disciples and grow the church numerically. My argument does not suggest that making disciples (the Great Commission) is anti-church growth. The focus of ministry is the real issue. On what do we base our definition of ministry success? I encourage the reader to consider this question. Is your notion of ministry the right or best way to define success? God knows the answer, so seek God before you reply.

Matthew 20:20-28 seems to be a fitting way to conclude this conversation. The mother of James and John brought them before Jesus and asked that Jesus grant each son a seat at Jesus' right and left hands in his kingdom. This great teaching moment produced those wonderful words that provide us with a level for judging the integrity of our motives and ministry goals: the one who would be great must become the servant. Amen.

Next Steps

- Talk with a career/vocational/mental health counselor about balance.

- Periodically create a "Ministry Satisfaction Checklist or Journal." Document the things you like about your work. Document the things that you could do without in the position. Be sure to list the reasons for each.

- Maintain a devotional life that keeps you in touch with God. Do not restrict yourself to one devotional activity. Hear God in as many ways as you can (e.g., meditation, quiet walks, prayer, etc.).

Questions TO CONSIDER

1. How do you define success in ministry? Write your responses.

2. Who are the successful ministers that you respect? What makes them successful to you?

3. Think of the future. Where will your successful ministry take place?

CHAPTER 10

Nurturing the Next Generation

Every year in November, I meet with Dr. David Daniels, Professor of Church History at McCormick Theological Seminary. During our meeting, we catch up on life and talk about the "Now what?" Dr. Daniels took time to meet with me during the early days of my postgraduate education. I had an idea of what to do for my PhD dissertation but needed guidance. I drove to Chicago one summer day in 2003 to have a conversation with him, and he has been a primary mentor for me ever since. He always makes time to speak with me. He cares about me as a person. And I have never paid for a meal when meeting with him. On one occasion, I offered to pay for our meal. He declined my offer, grabbed the check, and told me that someone did the same thing for him. Then he encouraged me to do the same for whomever I mentor.

The longer you live in your call, the more you learn about it. You will become a seasoned veteran in time. With that comes one of the biggest responsibilities a minister has—nurturing the next generation of leaders. I am expressing the essence of the Fund for Theological Education's (FTE) ministry. Its ministry to the world has been the cultivation of leadership for congregational and academic ministry settings. FTE provides resources for people who are living into their call in various ways. The fund has programs for seminarians, congregations, and people pursuing doctorates in theology and religious studies. FTE's goal has been to create an environment that will celebrate the call of people in ministry.

Be Aware of the Called among Us

A vital aspect of this nurture is discernment. During your years of ministry service, you will encounter all kinds of people and will sense the gifts and passions others have for ministry. At times you will identify people in need of guidance. For example, I am drawn to individuals who ask questions—implied or expressed. I am not referring to just any questions. I listen for the questions that ask for the meaning behind the meaning. On the first day of class, I invite students to share with me their expectations of the course. One person asked, "Why Christianity?" The premise behind the question was simple: there are many religions in the world; what makes Christianity such a prominent force—the right religion? I asked that student to talk with me after class. I wanted to create a safe space for her to develop responses to the question. She is now in the process of applying to a program that studies world religions.

Each of us has different ways of discerning the needs people have for ministry formation. The important thing to do is develop the discerning eye. If you are not able to meet a person's formation needs, invite others to help. That takes some discernment as well. A person can approach the task in more than one way.

Create a Culture of the Call

At some point, you might have "the talk." A potential minister may come to you and ask, "How did you know that you were called to ministry?" This is a wonderful moment! I approached Reverends William Badger, Ron Greer, Larry Jackson, and Clifton Williams in this way. They were associate ministers at Mt. Zion Baptist Church in Madison, Wisconsin. This was the translation to that question: "I've been called, now what?" The unscripted drama begins at that moment, so you must have a feel for how to approach it. The space to talk and work through questions can make all the difference in the world for a new minister.

These moments are invaluable for many reasons. They encourage and affirm our call, and they celebrate collegiality and relationships. Sharing yourself with a new minister gives rise to the "culture of the call." It provides the space and presence that can nurture the next generation of ministers. You can make this space over a meal, as Dr. Daniels has long done for me. The physical space is less important than the emotional and spiritual space for asking questions, discerning God's presence, and listening attentively and compassionately to one another. The key for creating the culture of the call is the intentional task of making time for questions. Following are a few examples.

Discernment Groups

Creating a discernment group is probably easier in the church than in other institutions. After all, how many other institutions or organizations throw around the word *discernment* so freely? There are ways to form a discernment group that may appeal to the people in your ministry context. A "seekers group" for young adults or several sessions for the youth ministry may start the process. Hold an information session on ministry as full-time vocation. The number of people who attend may surprise you.

High school students preparing for college leave for school curious about their next steps in life. What can you do to raise awareness of God's call to the ministry? Help them gain clarity about full-time ministry. Using books such as Alice Cullinan's *Sorting It Out: Discerning God's Call to Ministry* (Judson Press, 1999) can assist you in this endeavor. Or talk about call as a broader vocational journey. God can work with and through lawyers, sanitation workers, doctors, teachers, transit workers, and landscapers. It is a special privilege for called and discerning ministers to participate in discernment activities with others.

The discernment group can also help give meaning to the young adult experience in church settings. I attend several Christian education functions, conferences, and conventions each year. I have noticed in many settings a lack of young adult involvement. The few young adults I see at many of these events are ministers. While the suggestion for the discernment group is fostering a space for the call to full-time ministry, more can result from it.

Pool of Mentors

As mentioned above, there are organizations that act as mentors and facilitators for ministry formation and leadership development. Rev. Stephen Lewis, President of the Fund for Theological Education, was the organization's national director of the Calling Congregations Initiative. He and other members of the FTE staff would travel across the country doing workshops and conferences for new ministers and the congregations that affirm those calls. The Calling Congregations program is unique in its attempt to help local church congregations create a culture of the call. The Lilly Endowment's Academy of Preachers supports young people who are led to the gospel ministry. The Academy's Festival of Young Preachers is a celebration of the initiative and an opportunity to mentor and affirm the call. A number of young preachers from all parts of the United States attended the first event in January 2011.[1] All reports suggest that the initiative is healthy and growing.

Dr. Trinette McCray, former president of ABCUSA, created a website/blog to encourage the cultivation of ministry.[2] Other organizations attempt to do the same thing. Why? Gifted people sometimes need the nod to go forward and turn the world upside down.

Ministers-in-Training Programs

You may be more proactive and develop a Minister-in-Training program. Discerning the need for a broader approach to preparing for ministry can help the ministers at your church. This is also an opportunity to nurture the newly licensed ministers in your church. The program can include classes, workshops, and one-on-one mentoring, and can emphasize conversations about and resources on sermon development, biblical research, church administration, etc. Whether the training program is limited to six to ten weeks or is an ongoing educational tool, ministers will grow from such an intentional approach to ministry matters.

Support the Calls

The advocacy and nurture you offer do not have to end with the activities described above. Prevailing attitudes and customs disqualify certain groups from ministry leadership. Over time, women in ministry have experienced the brunt of discriminatory practices. Although many churches now embrace women in ministry, some still question the "spiritual" legitimacy of women in leadership. The subtle but present structure of ministerial hiring searches can sometimes leave called and qualified women out of pastoral applicant pools, because the committees cannot wrap their minds around the thought of a woman serving as the pastoral leader. In some cases, women must start congregations due to such call processes. All things being equal (or more accurately, unequal), a man may be the preference. Depending on where you are on this subject theologically, I encourage you to consider a couple of ways to correct this matter. (These tips will apply to certain contexts more than they will to others.)

First, congregations can invite a woman to preach on Sundays other than Women's Day. In some settings, the only time a congregation sees a woman preacher is at a gendered event such as this. Men preach every other "big" event in the life of the church. Perception can define reality. Such invitations suggest that the female preacher is only good for a themed sermon on women. Second, be the leader that initiates a conversation about women in ministry. Some of us want to address the controversial topics that exist in ministry. Advocacy is a part of our ministry. How do we do it? As a part of the informal ministry placement process I addressed in chapter 7, we can suggest all gifted and qualified people. As we offer names to search committee members, let us offer qualified men *and* women.

I have suggested that we nurture the next generation of people in ministry in several ways. We have opportunities to develop spaces and correct customs that will change the environment for ministry. The little girl or boy growing up in the pew will have the resources available to hear God call.

Questions TO CONSIDER

1. What are some things that your congregation can put in place to nurture the next generation of church leaders?

2. What are some practices that you feel will help create a culture of call in your context?

NOTES

1. For more information, see www.fteleaders.org and www.academyof preachers.net.

2. Trinette McCray, "A Culture of Call: The Calling of All God's People," *Minister Magazine* 32, no. 3 (2009): 13–14. www.ministerscouncil.org/Periodicals/documents/minmag0911.pdf.

Conclusion

The minister's work and service are similar to the cycle of seasons on earth. At this point in my life, I have come to recognize this seasonal nature of ministry. My vocational calendar as an apprentice minister started with licensing. It continued with my seminary and graduate education. The first full-time placement in the seminary classroom was another season. That season will extend to other places of ministry until eventually I will retire in some form or another.

Navigating this vocational calendar requires the same type of consideration we give to climate changes, from winter to spring. The minister's vocation begins with the budding vegetation of ministry potential. The summer, so to speak, of the career in ministry is that flurry of activity and/or transition. It is the desire to go out and do. Autumn comes to let us know that winter is around the corner, so prepare for change in activity. An unusually warm day may show up here and there in this season, but remember that the frost is approaching. And the winter is that time in the minister's vocational journey in which it is time to slow down. This season will prepare the ground for emerging buds and new life. And what will come in the seasons that follow are blessed opportunities to give, learn, share, and love.

This book has been my attempt to provide an overview of the spring and summer of the ministry journey. This book covers just the beginning of a new minister's journey. We have examined some of the critical ministry questions that one faces in the early stages of ministry. It is my hope that you have the accountability partners in ministry to keep the conversation going. The book, then, will accomplish what I intended it to do. Amen.

Sample Interview Questions

Are you an ordained minister in our denomination (PCUSA, UMC, UCC, AME, etc.)?

Tell us your story. Share with us your journey to the ministry.

What do you see as your strengths in ministry? What are some of the areas of your ministry that you need to grow or improve?

When did you know that God called you to pastor? What made you so sure about this idea?

How has your education and experience prepared you for the pastoral position?

The work of a pastor is very important to us. How would you define the position? What is the most important aspect of the pastor's ministry?

How much experience do you have with supervising and managing a staff?

We only have ___ staff member(s). How would you determine the need for more/fewer staff people? Which position would you hire/cut first? Why?

What are some necessary characteristics of a church staff member?

When you look at the changes to the culture of ministry, what innovations should remain? What are some questionable practices that might be unnecessary?

What is your opinion of technology in the church? How should we use it?

What are some best practices that churches should integrate in their worship experience? Why do you think they are successful?

Why did you leave your last ministry position?

What is your relationship with the people in your previous place of ministry?

What is your ministry vision for engaging and attracting new believers to this church?

How much experience do you have with leading a diverse ethnic and racial congregation?

How many languages do you speak? How willing are you to communicate with other ethnic populations?

Please give us some examples of your formal ministry to the community of your current church.

What are your views on women in ministry? What Scripture supports your position?

What are your views on certain sexual orientations and preferences? What Scripture supports your position?

If this is your first ministry position, how will you offset your inexperience?

This is a position of high moral integrity. Have you ever been arrested? What were the charges?

Please describe your current sermon preparation process.

What are your research sources? How do you plan for each week, month, and year? How much time do you spend per day/week? Do you prepare a manuscript or use note cards?

Describe your style of preaching/teaching (e.g., expository, thematic, use of drama or visual aids, classroom style, etc.).

What is your teaching philosophy?

What are your preaching/teaching goals when coming to a new congregation?

With what size crowd are you more comfortable—small groups or large crowds?

What is the central theme that your sermons cover each year?

What has been your experience with organizational or church budgets?

What is your position on church debt?

What is the state of your financial health?

What steps do you take to be a healthy person?

What do you do for recreation and relaxation?

What are some of your devotional practices?

What is your understanding of tithing? Should members tithe if they are in debt?

While maintaining confidentiality, please give examples of difficult counseling situations. How did you handle these situations?

What are the principles that you follow when conflict occurs? How do you attempt to reconcile varied positions?

What is your perspective on these issues?
- Teenage pregnancies
- Alcohol or drug addiction
- Politics and religion

With which group are you most comfortable: same-gender loving couples, children, youth, college/career, singles, young and married, men, women, seniors, street people (homeless), people in rehab, etc.? What have been your successes with these groups?

What is the major emphasis or passion of your ministry? What is the strongest part of your ministry (e.g., preaching, teaching, leadership, innovating, organizing, planning, handling finances, evangelizing, discipling, etc.)?

Define the mission of a local church.

What is the importance of a denomination? How will you maintain our denominational ties?

Please feel free to share anything else that you would like for us to know about you.

Sample Questions for the Search Committee

What are your expectations for an incoming minister/pastor?

Please describe the congregation's strengths. What are some of the "growing edges" that it needs to improve?

What is the church's relationship with other local congregations?

What kind of partnership does the church have with a denomination?

Please list some examples of the support you give for the pastor's continuing education.

What do you see as the congregation's major challenges?

How well do the ministries of the church support and complement each other?

In what ways does the church's location influence the way you perceive its mission? How does the church's budget reflect that perception? How do you carry out this mission?

How would you describe the membership?

What is your policy on pastoral sabbatical study leaves?

What are some of the unique challenges that this congregation faces?

How would you describe the theological bent of the congregation in relation to social and theological issues? What degree of diversity is there among the beliefs and convictions of the members on controversial issues?

Sample Church Description

River Rock Church
123 Main Street
Smallville, USA 12345

The River Rock Church began its ministry in 1878. We have a resident membership of about 400 people and average Sunday attendance of about 110 people. We seek a pastoral leader who appreciates the congregation's traditions and customs. We also desire that the person integrate contemporary practices. The congregation focuses on education. In 1997 the church added a library and twelve Christian education classrooms. The River Rock Church has had an important place in the life of this community for over 100 years. The membership believes that it is vital to call people to a personal faith commitment to Christ and equip people to grow together in Christ. Declining membership has increased the church's necessity for visionary leadership.

Sample Cover Letter

Today's Date

Pulpit Search Committee
River Rock Church
123 Main Street
Smallville, USA 12345

Dear Pulpit Search Committee:

I am writing in reference to your employment description for senior pastor at the River Rock Church. I am ordained in the Protestant Church Denomination (June 1999) and remain committed to the ministry of the denomination. I serve as an assistant pastor at the Mt. Horeb Church. My ministry consists of communicating with and developing programs for the membership through fourteen congregational ministries. I have also worked to recruit and advise high school and college students in our congregation. The pastor, moreover, invites me to preach on the third Sunday of each month. I work closely with her to provide relevant and healthy ministries to this six-hundred-member congregation.

I am a college and seminary graduate. My seminary experience helped me appreciate the emerging technology in church settings. A part of my responsibility at the church has been the development of practices that integrate some technology. We have done this while maintaining the integrity of our traditions. I have challenged myself to make theory and practice come together. I received aid in this task through my work with my home congregation. Recently I have served as chief strategist for the development of a new church-wide educational curriculum. Our achievements include the growth of key ministries in the church. We added a discipleship ministry to respond to the needs of people who are not familiar with the faith statements and mission of the church—denominational and universal.

I understand that education is an important aspect of the church's ministry. Therefore, I see the church as a place where disciples receive the knowledge necessary to accomplish the goals that Christ has set before us. I have used my gifts for teaching in Christian education forums and through written materials. For example, I teach continuing education courses in my congregation and a Sunday school class for teenagers. I recently published an article in the *Sunday Life: A Fictional Magazine* and produced Sunday school curriculum for the Mt. Horeb congregation.

Enclosed please find a current copy of my curriculum vita. If you should have any questions, please feel free to call me at 123-456-7890. You may also reach me by email at minister@minister.min. I would embrace the opportunity to learn more about River Rock. I would be glad to meet with you for an interview at your convenience. I look forward to hearing from you soon.

Sincerely,

Sample Thank-You Letter

Today's Date

Committee Member Smith
River Rock Church
123 Main Street
Smallville, USA 12345

Dear Committee Member Smith:

Thank you for interviewing me in these final stages of your pastoral search. The on-site interview provided me with an opportunity to see how I might fit into the ministry of the church. The experience strengthened my interest in being a part of the River Rock Church community. Thank you for arranging time for me to meet with several members of the church. I appreciated the warm and encouraging spirits of the committee members, youth group, evangelism ministry, and music department.

I feel that my ministry interests and concerns for the urban community are compatible with the mission of the church. River Rock is a place where I can grow as a person, minister, teacher, and social advocate. I feel confident that I am a minister who complements the current ministries of the church. I am eager to provide the leadership that the congregation needs at this point in its life.

Please contact me if the committee has any other questions or concerns. I look forward to hearing from you. Thank you for your time and consideration of the matter.

Sincerely,

Recommended Resources

Vocation and Calling

Cullinan, Alice R. *Sorting It Out: Discerning God's Call to Ministry.* Valley Forge, PA: Judson, 1999.

LaReau, Renee M. *Getting a Life: How to Find Your True Vocation.* Maryknoll, NY: Orbis, 2003.

LaRue, Cleophus J., ed. *This Is My Story: Testimonies and Sermons of Black Women in Ministry.* Louisville: Westminster John Knox, 2005.

Myers, William H. *God's Yes Was Louder Than My No: Rethinking the African American Call to Ministry.* Grand Rapids: Eerdmans, 1994.

Palmer, Parker J. *Let Your Life Speak: Listening for the Voice of Vocation.* San Francisco: Jossey-Bass, 1999.

Placher, William C., ed. *Callings: Twenty Centuries of Christian Wisdom on Vocation.* Grand Rapids: Eerdmans, 2005.

Schuurman, Douglas J. *Vocation: Discerning Our Callings in Life.* Grand Rapids: Eerdmans, 2003.

Stevens, R. Paul. *The Other Six Days: Vocation, Work, and Ministry in Biblical Perspective.* Grand Rapids: Eerdmans, 2000.

Walker, Riley, and Marcia Patton. *When the Spirit Moves: A Guide for Ministers in Transition.* Valley Forge, PA: Judson, 2011.

The Work of the Church series. Valley Forge, PA: Judson. Various titles, including *The Work of the Pastor, The Work of the Chaplain, The Work of the Bivocational Minister,* and *The Work of the Associate Pastor.*

Ordination

Brackney, William H. "Ordination in the Larger Baptist Tradition." *Perspectives in Religious Studies* 29, no. 3 (2002): 225–39.

Hinson, E. Glenn. "Ordination in Christian History." *Review and Expositor* 78, no. 4 (1981): 485–96.

Lynch, John E. "Ordination of Women: Protestant Experience in Ecumenical Perspective." *Journal of Ecumenical Studies* 12, no. 2 (1975): 173–97.

Sprinkle, Stephen V. *Ordination: Celebrating the Gift of Ministry.* St. Louis, MO: Chalice, 2004.

Willimon, William H. *Calling and Character: Virtues of Ordained Life.* Nashville: Abingdon, 2000.

Zikmund, Barbara Brown. "The Protestant Women's Ordination Movement." *Union Seminary Quarterly Review* 57, no. 3–4 (2003): 123–45.

Seminary

Cetuk, Virginia Samuel. *What to Expect in Seminary: Theological Education as Spiritual Formation.* Nashville: Abingdon, 1998.

Cooper, Derek. *So You're Thinking about Going to Seminary: An Insider's Guide.* Grand Rapids: Brazos, 2008.

Core, Deborah. *The Seminary Student Writes.* St. Louis, MO: Chalice, 2000.

Parker, Ronald E. *Do I Belong in Seminary?* Herndon, VA: Alban Institute, 1998.

Websites

www.abc-usa.org	American Baptist Churches USA
www.ame-church.org	African Methodist Episcopal Church
www.amez.org	African Methodist Episcopal Zion Church
www.ccdmin.org	Center for Career Development and Ministry
www.disciples.org	Christian Church (Disciples of Christ)
www.thefellowship.org	Cooperative Baptist Fellowship
www.elca.org	Evangelical Lutheran Church of America
www.nationalbaptist.com	National Baptist Convention USA, Inc.
www.nbcainc.com	National Baptist Convention of America
www.pcusa.org	Presbyterian Church USA
www.pnbc.org	Progressive National Baptist Convention
www.sbc.net	Southern Baptist Convention
www.ucc.org	United Church of Christ
www.umc.org	United Methodist Church